MY FORTUNATE LIFE

DR. GERRY FLACK

To Bridget
With much love & memories
of Hadleigh.
Yours ever
Gerry F.

A CIP catalogue record for this book is available from the British Library.

ISBN No.: 978-0-9935767-4-4

Printed and published in England by Mickle Print (Canterbury) Ltd
micklecreative.com

This book is dedicated to my wife, Trish,
my daughters, Caroline and Marianne,
sons Johnny and Will,
grandchildren, great-grandchildren
and our extended family.

FOREWORD

This autobiography is compiled from the transcripts of recordings of conversations with Gerry and Trish Flack between February 2013 and 2016. It is a faithful account of Gerry's life, as spoken by him and Trish. It is valuable for being in his own words, which are conversational and unpretentious.

For people who know him, the way Gerry has told his story will bring to mind the man, his way of speaking and his kindly manner. To others it will be understandable as it is and will give a flavour of the personality of this country Doctor in the early days of the National Health Service, the changing character of the country immediately post war and the changing nature of medical practice as it feels its way towards the 21st century.

His unusual childhood, brought up by a lone parent who he only saw at long intervals and a surrogate family who informally adopted him between boarding school terms, is quite exotic and of its era. It puts into context his deep empathy with people of every description and his wish to do everything possible to help them, as a fellow man as much as a physician.

The picture of life in London as a medical student immediately post war; the more informal way of bringing up a young family with the involvement of friends and neighbours; his activities as a member of the territorial army; all evoke the era.

The emphasis in all Gerry's stories is on the personal but with a view to the historical. He has chosen to describe things which highlight changes in social history, including the developing health service as well as the evolution of a village from a farming community with an agricultural college at its heart to a bigger, more impersonal small town.

CONTENTS

Above left: Father, Benjamin James Henry Flack (left), Ibadan, Nigeria.

Above right: 'The Oyo of Ife' (Ben Flack), Ibadan, in local dress.

Left: Father, Ben Flack (3rd from left) Royal West Africa Frontier Force volunteers 1938/9.

Below: Father, Ben Flack (5th from left) 'Comptable', United Africa Company (later Uniilever).

CHAPTER 1: CHILDHOOD

My father, Benjamin Flack, who was born in Newcastle, came from a large family. His father had married again and when the war came in 1914, like a lot of youngsters, it was a glorious opportunity to escape. He had got a place in Grammar School, but there was a lack of support from his family, who thought he should go out to work. He hopped it and joined the local Fusiliers' regiment. His mother then came along with his birth certificate and, because he was only 16, got him out. So the next time he went further afield and he joined the Wiltshire Regiment in Salisbury and off he went. He served in the First World War and was wounded. He came out of the war in 1920 as a Regimental Quartermaster Sergeant, so he obviously had a gift for organisation of some sort – and survival. He always told me that the only wound that he had was a broken nose where he had been kicked by a mule. He had, however, holes in the back of legs and he had been gassed. He then joined the United African Company, Unilever, and went to Nigeria where he served until 1944 when he came back home, seriously ill.

Mother, Amy Flack (nee Robinson) in the 1920s

I think that he had three months leave every 18 months and, during the course of one of them, he got himself engaged to a girl; but when he came back the next time she had pushed off with somebody else. He had, however, made very good friends with her sister and brother-in-law, and when he came back on leave, they took pity on him and they had a great friendship.

On one of his leaves, in about 1928, he became engaged to Amy Robinson, aged 24, married and took his bride back to Africa – which was a thing that you did not do then – it was known as 'the white man's grave'. I have pictures which are quite interesting which have a sea of faces and scribbled on the back it says, 'Can you see me? I am the only one there.' That was a picture of my mother, who was white, among a sea of black faces. I was conceived in Nigeria and wisely she came home to have me. I was born in Stretford Memorial Hospital, Manchester, next door to the Cricket Ground, in 1929.

My mother stayed in England until I was about 18 months and then, after the next leave that my Father had, went back with him, leaving me behind with her sister, Auntie Bertha, which, as far as I know, was fine. My mother conceived again and once more came back to have the baby, but unfortunately got malaria and blackwater fever, was taken off the boat at Le Havre and died in France. I have never bothered to follow this up - my father was not keen on telling me about it. I suppose I did want to know, but I felt that I was delving into something rather painful. It is only recently that my children found out that my mother was taken from Le Havre and buried in Manchester along with her baby child. So I had a brother that I never knew about, and they are buried in a Manchester churchyard side by side. I never knew about this until my family found out.

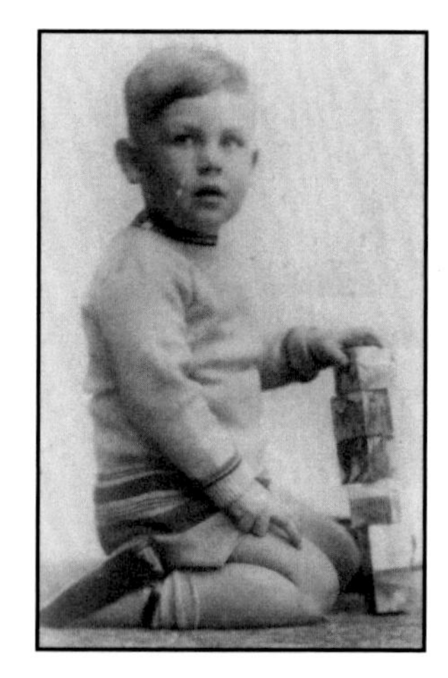

Me in 1932, Weymouth, soon after my mother's death

My father was then left with no wife and a son, but Aunt Bertha carried on looking after me until she met a chap and got married and he was not enthusiastic about taking on somebody else's child, not even his wife's sister's child. My father managed to find the wife of one of his work colleagues to look after me as a paying guest in Weymouth, and then he returned to Africa on his own.

My earliest memories of lodging in Radipole, near Weymouth, were when my father visited me on leave from Africa. I was sitting on my pot in the loo when a strange man came in and had a pee! It must have been the husband of the lady I was lodged with. It made a strong impression on me. The old Great Western Railway was nearby and I remember when (aged five to seven) there were two big steam trains converted with a bullet front. I also remember when we went to the railway station I saw pigeon baskets waiting to be opened for races. They had lead seals that had to be broken before they were released, to prevent cheating.

Me, with my father (in leopard skin) on leave, Nab Wood 1933

My father's job in Africa was the only job he had ever had and I think that his income was quite reasonable and helped to support me in boarding school. The colleague's wife had three sons of her own so I was there as number four in the family, and we lived in what was probably rented accommodation because there was an old lady, Miss Selby, living in the top floor of the house and I think that it was her property. She was a nice old lady. I used to escape up to her. She gave me a book of Fairy Tales, which I still have. It was not a happy household. I was the odd one out. I was the cuckoo in the nest. But I had escapes - Miss Selby was an escape. It was not an easy situation there, to say the least of it. I was aged four then and when I was old enough, I think about five, I went as a boarder to Weymouth College.

Strangely enough, years later, when I was here (in Kent), I got called to a temporary resident, who said that he lived in Weymouth and was a farmer. And, blow me down, when I said, 'Where do you live in Weymouth?' he said, 'Icen Road.' I said, 'So did I, in Number 45,' and he said 'then you are Gerald!' I used to sneak over there and go to the farm. He remembered me. It was extraordinary. His name was Pocock, a local name, but that was years later.

I saw my father every 18 months. I remember each time he came we would go somewhere – we just travelled around when I was young, I do not remember exactly where; we used to go to Manchester, obviously, to see Auntie Bertha, and to Newcastle. Each time he was on leave there was a trip, but, unfortunately, on one of the particular trips, I managed to break my leg badly. I was aged five or six then. I had been big enough to throw a ball into a big urn thing and in an attempt to retrieve it, the urn fell on me and I ended up in hospital for nearly all of my Father's leave. He visited me every night. That was his leave really, keeping coming to see me in hospital. I knew when he was coming in because he was always whistling the same tune, 'When I Grow too Old to Dream'.[i] The hospital was the one that I had been born in. They did not have children's wards in hospitals in those days and so I was in a male ward and people were very caring. I was there for a couple of months. I had to have an operation every fortnight to straighten my leg, as I had broken both the tibia and fibula and a lot of time was spent on me, so I was attracted to hospitals. Then I went back to Weymouth and had the plaster off there. I remember it being taken off and being very frightened to stand on my leg.

I remember the death of King George V and about that time there was an enormous epidemic of foot and mouth. I can still smell the burning corpses and looking out of my window seeing funeral pyres, all over the place. So this would be probably 1935/36. I also remember that from Weymouth, you could look across the bay. There was a big Naval Fleet then in Weymouth Bay with all the lights on, so I saw the Fleet lit up, I also remember seeing Sir Alan Cobham's Flying Circus (Air Show). This was the first time that I had seen aeroplanes; I think it was also 1935/36 – I would have been seven then. After that there was the abdication, and then King George VI was crowned.

Then my father came back one time and discovered that he had been two-timed by the family I was with; he was being charged for buying me new clothes, when I was having the family hand-me-downs. His money was not being spent on me; this was rumbled by one of his friends. My father did not know what to do, but his friend George Dixon said that they would have me, so they took me on. I was seven and a half. He and Aunty Kit (nee Drew) lived in Orpington and had a daughter, Pam, who was the same age as myself. In retrospect, they were as good to me as most people's parents and became my childhood family. In their later life, we looked after them. I had to change school, but was a boarder still; I went to Bedford Modern School. The school had three levels: junior, middle and senior. It was before the war in 1937 when I was aged 8. I was there throughout the war until I was 18. When I left in 1946 I was deputy head boy. Pam, my 'sister', was evacuated to Devon.

Top: Catherine (Kit) and George Dixon "guardians".

Above: Mad on aircraft - visit to Croydon airport with "Auntie Kit", 1939.

In 1939 a school called Owen School had to be evacuated to us. They ended up at Bedford Station, where they did not know what to do or where to go. Our Headmaster agreed to share our school with them, so we were two schools in one. We did lessons in the morning and then had sport and 'freedom' in the afternoon; they did the reverse. 'Freedom' involved agricultural work, when I saw for the first time a sheep with 'fly strike'. In the holidays we went to camps in such places as Anglesey, and Beaumaris Castle, the grounds of which had a moat full of eels. Once we watched a spitfire with floats taking part in a sea trial in the Menai strait.

At first, I was bullied at school as I was small and I was called 'Nipper'. I had a temper which rarely came out, but when provoked it led to me fighting. As usual, the instigators got away scot free but I was always in trouble and this sometimes led to corporal punishment from senior boys and masters alike. When I became Head of Hall, I put a stop to senior boys inflicting corporal punishment and also fagging. I was the only boy allowed to give beatings and, of course, I never did.

I had holidays always in Orpington, which was fine. My Father came back in 1940 from West Africa for his leave and then he did not come back again

until 1944 because there was no way of getting back. Then, you can guess, at school, other pupils knew the name of the boat that my father was on because I told them and they said, 'Oh yes, it has been sunk' - schoolboys can be little sods. I did not know one way or the other until I heard that he had arrived in Nigeria in 1944. He had, however, been invalided back in as he was very ill. He had pulmonary tuberculosis and all kinds of chest troubles which eventually killed him.

At school, I was in the Officer Training Corps (OTC) to start with and then, as the Air Training Corps (ATC), sounded a bit more romantic, I swapped. When I got my 1st Fifteen Rugby colours, a teacher called Mr Protheroe gave me a blazer that had belonged to his son who had been killed in Crete. These were unobtainable elsewhere at that time. We were thrashed by Loughborough College on one occasion, but this was because their team was made up of hardened ex-servicemen who had returned from the war. I remember that there were three German refugees in the boarding house at the school – they were Jewish. One of them, named Lidstein, later came back to visit the school. I also remember that at school there were two sexual predators, who would nowadays have ended up in court, but they were just 'removed'.

Top: Me (2nd left) known as Nipper, Stamford House, Bedford 1939.

Above: Me and "sister" Pam in school holidays, Petts Wood 1939.

Below: Officer Training Corps, Bedford Modern School 1939.

At Bedford I leaned towards the sciences. I do not know why. I have many regrets that I did move towards the sciences because the arts were neglected rather. I have a feeling that my Father must have influenced something in me early on because people seemed to think that I was going to be a doctor even then. Possibly the time that I had in hospital when I had my broken leg had something to do with it. I was spoiled rotten there. There was no past history at all of doctors in the family. Although funnily enough, if you look in the medical directory, there are quite a lot of Flacks. There is a part of the heart named after Keith and Flack (the node of Keith and Flack) and Lambert Flack was on the BMA Committee.

I had to do a couple of languages at school. I had the greatest of difficulty with languages to be quite honest. Latin was pushed on me and French - you needed Latin for medicine. I had to have two goes at Latin in my School Certificate and eventually got it. You had to get a Matriculation, which was so many subjects in one go - 5 credits. I had a very good biology master who was not exactly an easy man, but he was good and taught very well.

On VE Day in 1945, some of us broke out and climbed over the wall and joined in the local celebrations that were going on. When we climbed back over the wall again into the school, we saw the lighted cigar of our housemaster, Billy Belcher, waiting the other side. Although he caught us coming back, he took no action.

I went for an interview at St. Thomas' and Guy's Medical School, London. The interviews were undertaken by the Bursar, Colonel Crockford. The questions were: 'Do you play Rugger?' – 'Yes'. 'What position?' – 'Scrum half' and a discussion about Rugby form – and that was it. In order to secure your place to study Medicine, and your first MB exemption, you had to get Physics, Chemistry, Botany and Zoology at a decent pass level for Higher School Certificate. I failed my Physics. I had already got the place at St. Thomas' and Guy's, but having failed Physics I could not get in to the first MB exemption, so National Service then loomed. It would have been deferred until after qualification, had I got into medical school, and then you would have become an army doctor, automatically. I chose St Thomas' because they contacted me while in the army and kept me a place!

Top: Sportsman - school rowing team (cox, centre), 1945

Left: School cross-country team (front, 3rd left) 1945

CHAPTER 2: NATIONAL SERVICE 1947 TO 1949

National Service lasted for two years and I went straight from school to the army. The army was very considerate because one of the things that they asked was, 'Have you got any relations who are ill?' and presumably somewhere in my records they had this. My father had to have a lot of surgery and he spent most of his time in convalescent homes but when he became well enough he became a paying guest with various people they called 'Coasters' who were West African – United African Service men. He was in and out of hospital a lot, which of course you then paid for as there was no National Health Service. He had surgery performed by a man called Sir Thomas Holmes Sellors (1902 – 1987)[ii], who was the chest surgeon of his day. He used to put ping-pong balls in the lungs to press the lung down. The fact that my Father had TB immediately made the army suspicious that I might have it, so I had to go through all types of tests before they admitted me.

I did National Service in this country. I moved around, but was kept local and I like to think that was because they were charitable. My call-up was to the Royal Fusiliers at Hounslow Barracks in London. One of the first duties I was given was to be sent off to do inoculations for men going off on their first leave, so that if any of them reacted to the vaccines, they could be ill at home, rather than at the Barracks. Most of my contemporaries there were Barrow Boys. I learnt a lot there because many of them were illiterate and I spent a lot of time reading and writing their letters for them. It was an experience that one would not have had going straight from school into the hospital. Then I opted for the Artillery after the initial training. I went to the 'ack-ack' regiment at Stoneleigh near Birmingham, (now the Stoneleigh Park Show Ground). With a name like Flack it was obvious that the regiment that I joined there was the 'ack-ack'.

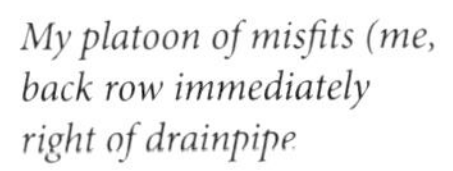

My platoon of misfits (me, back row immediately right of drainpipe

Joining the artillery was quite interesting. Three others and myself were sent to a little unit in Lode Lane, Solihull in 1947. This is very easy to date because I saw only yesterday that Land Rover were advertising that they started in 1947, which was exactly when I was there and next to the gun-site that I was on, there was the Land Rover track. Day and night they were driving these cars to destruction on a circuit with pave, mud, hills and so on, and they were just going round and round and round, on and on and on. I had the pleasure of looking after German prisoners of war there. They used to come every day in a bus to put up a fence round the guns because the camp site had been taken over by squatters, all bar the one place that we were in. They used to come in to put a cage around the guns that the kids had been playing on. This was after the war when people were homeless and squatters were everywhere. There were Nissen huts in the gun site. The job of the Germans was also to fence this area to keep the squatters out. We were in the Gatehouse and the Sergeants' Mess which was fenced off. There were the three of us in the Gatehouse, but we were allocated rations for seven, so we were able to bribe the Germans, via their officer in charge, with the surplus.

I did not get on with the Sergeant Major at the unit, so as I was destined to go to medical school, I went before the War Officer Selection Board at Catterick and was deemed officer material. I went for officer training to escape the Sergeant Major. When I was made a Lance Bombardier, he was rid of me from the camp site.

National Service Training. Mons Barracks, Aldershot (me 2nd row, 2nd right) 1948

I went for officer training school at Mons Barracks, near Aldershot; a sort of junior Sandhurst. I learnt a lot there. Our Regimental Sergeant Major (RSM) was quite famous, RSM Britton, who had all kinds of wonderful, colourful language. He was a very straight guy. He would walk along inspecting and stand behind somebody and say 'Am I hurting you?' 'No sir'. 'I should be. I am standing on your back hair. Get your hair cut!' I also had the ignominy of being taken off parade for a ghastly mistake in my drill and stuck in the Guard House, boots off, shoelaces out and the rest of it. I had turned left instead of right. But after the Passing Out Parade, which my father managed to come to, RSM Britton made a point of taking my father to the Sergeant's Mess, as he had been a Sergeant, and looked after him.

Whilst in the army I was involved in a very unfortunate route march, which was an event for all the groups at the officer training corps at Mons. You had to go on a graduated mileage series of bashes. This one was a six-mile bash which you were supposed to do in an hour; the idea was to try to get the record. It was around the time of the 1948 Olympics - the hottest summer for years. It was not just a bit of a warm day, it was absolutely a heat wave and no arrangements had been made for any support. Only five of us finished it and three blokes died. You can look that up on the internet somewhere[iii]. We were dressed in full kit, tin hats with rifles, no water, not a thing, and you did not stop. A long part of it was along the tow path of the Basingstoke Canal, and so not only was it hot but the humidity was great. The guys just dropped out because they could not go the distance. The establishment covered it up very well. It was suppressed, but all personnel involved were demoted and one was sacked. It was interesting that the guys who finished it – I was one of them – had been busy training for some athletic activities in the previous two or three weeks, so we were fit – comparatively fit. But I must admit that I have never ever felt so exhausted in my life – and for days afterwards. We were suddenly posted a week early for gunnery training elsewhere. The only guys left behind were the 'yes-boys' who wouldn't make trouble. That whole episode did give me an 'attitude'.

I was very tempted to stay in the army. I loved it and got on all right there. It suited me and I found it easy. It was far easier than the experience of boarding at boarding school. Also you get very close to people. I had the pleasure, after Commission, of going to a regiment on the Isle of Wight. Three of us had a gunnery battery - we had two batteries at HQ and one elsewhere, with each of us in charge as a Second Lieutenant Officer, which was the most junior rank. I was in a battery detached to Gosport, Portsmouth. One was a bloke called Roger Champion, one was Maurice Childs and the three of us have remained as friends, even now. Roger lives in Tenterden - he is our solicitor and was our

'My troop'. Fox troop (seated centre), Haslar Barracks, Gosport 1949

Best Man. We are godparents to each other's children.

Was it an option to stay in the army? I had got on quite well in there. It seemed a very good life, based largely in Portsmouth and the Isle of Wight. There was Cowes Week and lots of life and it was all very easy. The crunch came in October 1949. I had not got any funding to get into Medical School. I had applied for a County Grant and heard nothing back. So eventually I had to write to them and say that if I did not hear within the next day of so I would have to sign on with the army because I had nothing else to do. I did eventually get a letter saying, 'Yes, we will support you,' and I got a grant. I had done rather well in becoming a radar officer, which involved a lot of physics. There was a big exercise on at the time in 1949, which involved planning tactics for the next war, in which I was playing quite a valuable part. Then, in the middle of this important army exercise, I had to go and tell my Colonel, to get his permission to leave. He was absolutely furious and did not give me an easy time. I had a good life in the army because I played rugby, I played cricket and I sailed a lot because we were next door to Cowes. I used to sail Swallows and I had made lasting friendships.

CHAPTER 3: MEDICAL SCHOOL 1949

Having now been given a place at St Thomas' I had to spend a whole year taking one subject – Physics – nothing to do with medicine as far as I could see, but I had to take it as I had missed out on exemption for the first MB. (There was a Physics Department at St Thomas' as well as Biochemistry.) That nearly made me chuck in Medicine, but one of the people made me feel better about it and who influenced me a lot was a very good friend of mine called Hughes, who was a Doctor for the Southern Region Railway. He lived nearby and he was very helpful. All I did for a year was Physics, which meant that I had a lot of spare time. I could walk around and get to know London and go to museums and go to the theatre and so on. But I joined up with 'Doc Hughes' because he used to do a lot of examining for First Aid. The Railways are dead keen on First Aid, really enthusiastic. I would go round as his 'casualty' and pretend I had got something wrong with me. When we were in the First Class carriages, he called me 'Dr Flack'. I think Doc Hughes had a big influence on me. During that year, when I was not doing much, my grant was not very substantial and I needed to work to survive. I went to see the Professor of Anatomy, Professor Davis, and asked if I could do a bit of dissecting, or anything, because I had so much time on my hands. He was not too sure, but he said 'Yes, all right, come and see me next week,' which I did. He gave me a baby to dissect, when everybody else was dissecting adult bodies. I was stuck in a corner, just dissecting a baby. I think that he was trying to persuade me to give up. But I persisted, and although it was not a pleasant job it got me back into being interested in medicine.

As a medical student, St. Thomas' Hospital 1949

I think that I was given a Physics pass in the end so I could start proper Medicine. I felt quite strongly that it was all very well being at Medical School but there were other things in life. I found it a bit overwhelming just talking about Medicine all the time. So I joined the Territorial Army, resigned my Commission and joined the Honourable Artillery Company (HAC) but not as an officer. I started off as a gunner again and eventually rose to the exalted rank of a Gun Sergeant. I was based in the City. It was a very prestigious organisation and quite useful in many ways because there was some financial incentive. We paraded on Wednesdays and did one weekend a month plus two weeks' annual camping. We had quite long vacations in the first few years at medical school and it meant that I could go on a course of some sort, which included learning to drive tracked vehicles in the form of tanks. These courses were all paid for. You would also get a bounty at the end of it which was worth a lot of money, which was an incentive. It meant that one met people who were from all walks of life and the regiment was very liberal. The lines between ranks were very blurred unlike in the regular army where you knew exactly where you were. In the HAC it was not like that at all. Most of the guys were city people. There was nothing we liked better than driving tanks around Salisbury Plain as students - we all needed jobs to survive. My wife Trish says that I now drive a car as if I was driving a tank – with the seat crammed up against the steering wheel.

It was around this time in 1952 that my father died. He had been staying in one of the 'Coasters' houses in Lilleshall, near Newport, Shropshire and I had not been able to see a lot of him once I started my medical training. He was 54. I was often one of the HAC troops that always celebrated the Queen's birthdays and any national event requiring the 21 gun salutes. I also remember being on parade at George VI's funeral - we lined the street. The king had died in Norfolk and was sent to London by train. At Fenchurch Street station his body was put on a gun carriage and I was one of the hundreds of soldiers lining the route, which had been sanded. "Rest on your arms reversed," was the drill, with the muzzle of the gun on our boot and our heads bowed on the butt in respect. I can still hear the sound of the marching sailors who were pulling the gun carriage.

As a medical student I could get time off during the week, which other people could not. So I always managed to get away to fire the Royal Salute and Salutes for State Visits for people like Khrushchev or other visiting notables. They sometimes came up the Thames. The ceremonial guns were just ordinary 25 pounders. We used to get to the Armoury house in City Road at say 10.00am and then fix them on the back of our vehicles and drive down to Tower Green in the Tower of London. The Royal Horse Artillery do the proper thing in full military uniform. They were really efficient - we just amateurs in battle dress. I did that for about five years. Never had signs of deafness! One armistice Sunday I was detailed to go to a Remembrance Parade at the Gunner Memorial in Hyde Park. It was a miserable, wet day. Who should come along to inspect the eight or ten of us but Alan Brooke[iv], complete with bowler hat and umbrella. He had been the wartime army Chief of Staff. He spoke to each of us and thanked us individually. He was one of the few who stood up to Churchill.

Another thing that happened when I was a medical student was the flooding in Holland in 1953. I was with a group of medical students from St. Thomas' who flew out there to rescue people with inflatables and all sorts of equipment. We students had volunteered initially to go and help with the floods that had affected the east coast of England as well as the Isle of Sheppey but there had been a rapid response and we were not needed. One of my contemporaries had been a pilot in the war who had been helped by the Dutch Resistance Movement. He had a friend in the Dutch Embassy whom he contacted and said 'Can I be of any help?' His friend said 'Yes, we need volunteers. We are in chaos,' because Holland had been absolutely devastated. All the Zuiderzee had been devastated. Between us we had about four days to prepare.

The floods happened on a Saturday/Sunday night, and by the Tuesday, we were on an aeroplane to Holland, fully equipped with rubber boats, rations, etc. It all happened very quickly. It was all organised within the hospital by Noel Moynahan, who was the pilot. He went on to become a London doctor and I understand that he was Prudence Loudon's[v] doctor in London. We were out there for about a month from January 31st 1953. Off we went and arrived in Amsterdam, Schiphol Airport, and then went by boat to a town called

Sportsman - scrum half, Westcombe Park RFC (bottom row, 3rd left) 1951-52

Dordrecht, and then on to an island called Schouwen-Duiveland where we stayed for a month. By the time we got there everybody had been rescued so the most useful thing that we could do as medical students was to look for bodies – and that is what we spent our time doing. It was a daily job, in groups of three, going out in the morning in inflatables to search. The severe storms had broken down the sea-defences, called polders, and the reclaimed land again became tidal. We had rubber boats. The height of the water was to the top of barbed wire and, as it was February, it was bitterly cold. It was a very unfortunate time. A memory that is fixed in my mind is going with an old man to dig up his two children whom he had buried. He never found his wife, but he had found his two children. I remember him standing there with a drip on his nose – he had buried them himself and he took us to them - what did one do? I did not know a word of Dutch and he did not know English, there were three of us there trying to help. A hug speaks louder than words.

The United Nations of Europe turned up to help. There were troops from France using searchlights, making night become day. There were also American Officers with the Germans (who were their sort of proxy army). There was no German army but there was a 'Technical Corps' and they came with DUKWs (amphibious vehicles). The Islanders would not allow them anywhere near them. Quite early on, when they tried to help, the islanders refused to be rescued by them. They would sit on their roofs rather than be rescued. Also some of them would not be rescued on a Sunday on religious grounds. I was aged 23/24 and learnt a lot. The guys who I went with had all been in the forces so we all had experience.

When we were in Holland, a number of the people who were helping were billeted into the school at Zierikzee – all kinds of nationalities were there. In the middle of the night a drunken lot of Belgians appeared - I do not remember where they had come from. They had managed to sail in their fishing boat onto a polder, and when the tide went out, they were stranded on land. They had obviously been sloshed before being grounded. They all came in and were making one heck of a noise whilst we were all knackered and all we wanted to do was get our heads down in our three-tier bunks; it was bitterly cold. There were two English Marine Commandos who had spent the day diving to try to restore some lock gates into Zierikzee harbour. This noise went on and suddenly one of the marines jumped out of his sleeping bag waving a knife, saying, 'If you do not bloody well shut up I will have the lot of you.' The effect was total silence!

The actual town of Zierikzee had more or less escaped as it had been built on an island. In the town there was a campanile and I remember climbing up it to look at the countryside and found a music sheet on the top there; it was 'Home, Home on the Range'[vi]. After we came back, we went twice to the Dutch Embassy in London. The second time Trish came. There had been a junior member of the Embassy in 1953 who then became Ambassador to Britain. He invited us and wives to the Embassy 20 years later on. He gave us a large written tribute signed by Queen Juliana which she had sent us. The Dutch appreciated our help more than one can imagine.

It was an interesting time as a student because there were three student divisions. You were either very bright and got straight into Medical School at the age of 18; or you were not so bright, failed one exam or had a brush with the examiners; or you had gone into the forces first and done your national service. But then there was another group of students who served throughout the war, and they were aged 30 plus and would not stand any nonsense from the professors or anybody else. They had seen it all, (it was the same at Wye College with the mature students). In fact the oldest chap was a fellow aged over 60 who was a judge who had decided to become a missionary doctor. He had been in India. Women had only just become accepted as students. Another of my student colleagues, who was a contemporary in my year, was Cecily Saunders[vii]. She had been a nurse who decided to go in for medicine, became a doctor, and then founded the Hospice movement. Her particular friend at the time was Louise Vanier, who was a Consultant Haematologist, and later co-founded the L'Arche Community[viii]. We were an extraordinary group. I did not think about it at the time.

Towards the end of my training, we could be seconded anywhere. Possibly because my Father had TB, I took the opportunity of going to a TB Sanatorium in Midhurst to see what it was like. It was a very famous Sanatorium - they are all gone now, of course - but this was a very well known one and it was largely full of ex-service people at the time because it was just after the war. Leonard Cheshire[ix] was there - he had bi-lateral pulmonary TB. He had had surgery, by the same surgeon that my father had, actually. He'd had ribs removed and a thoracoplasty, and poor old Cheshire had got an infected space which had to be washed out every day with tubes pushed into the top of his lung. He was extraordinary. He had just started the Cheshire Homes and although he was hardly able to breathe, he was dictating his various talks about his Charity on one of these old tape recorders. He was having to do this about four words at a time. He would be doing this when one went in to wash his infected space out and he would stop and say, 'I am ready', and whereas everybody else had to have gas and air for their wash-outs, he did not have anything. He just used to go into a kind of trance and he always just sat there and then said 'thank you very much' and just carried on dictating his next talk. He just used to be able to relax himself. You could see that he was in pain, but was controlling it. He was that sort of chap.

He had been awarded a VC, two DSO's and goodness knows what for his flying as a bomber pilot throughout the war. He eventually became the original 'pathfinder' and he used to fly in before the bombers, dropping flares then guiding them in. He was also the number one bomber pilot during the war and the one selected from the English pilots to be present when the first Atom bomb was dropped. He was in the plane when it was dropped. It changed him - totally changed his life. He became devoted to dedicating his life to helping people. He started off by taking in refugees who had come over to England from Poland etc. after the war, and that is how it started. He was a wonderful chap.

CHAPTER 4: TRISH

I met Trish in 1952 when she was twenty. My father had died that February and I met her in the summer on what was really a sort of blind date. Trish was a trainee nurse at the Middlesex and I was doing medicine at St. Thomas'. A previous girlfriend called Jessica, who was also at the Middlesex and a year junior to Trish, invited me to this dance. I only replied yes the day before the ball - I was short of cash actually but decided to go because I had nothing better to do. Meanwhile she had found somebody else to go with, so there would have been three of us.

Trish was supposed to be going to the dance, but had cried off. She was working with Jessica, who said that she had got a party up to go to the ball and they were one person short – would she possibly fill in. 'No way,' said Trish, not wanting to go with a group of people she did not know. Anyway, Jessica went on and on and on until Trish said 'oh all right'. Also, Trish was supposed to be rehearsing that night with the United Hospitals Choir at the Victoria Drill Hall near the station - they were singing Elijah at the Albert Hall - so she had not been at all worried about missing this jolly dance. Anyway, Jessica finally persuaded her, but Trish was a bit fed up about it. She mentioned that she had invited someone called Nigel who sang in the choir with Trish, so Trish thought 'oh that is all right if Nigel is going, because I know him.'

Trish remembers that on the day of the ball she was playing in a tennis match at St. Bartholomew's. She came back from the tennis match exhausted and had a bath. So, she goes downstairs after her bath, all dressed up, and in the foyer of the nurses' home - a big foyer with a lot of settees all round it - she sees Jessica and a young man whom she had never clapped eyes on before. That was me! And to her astonishment Jessica let the cat out of the bag by saying 'oh well, I have invited a chap called Gerry Flack from St. Thomas'. I had asked him before, but he had not replied.' We then had to go to Victoria Drill Hall to pick up Nigel from the rehearsal. So how did we get there? We had to get a taxi and funds were running low but I coughed up for the taxi. We stood there listening to Elijah and then eventually when Nigel appeared we got into another taxi. Afterwards, I have never seen two people get out of a taxi faster than Nigel and Jessica on arrival and I was left with the second fare. So I was not best pleased by then. And then I was left with Trish. What do you do? So it was sort of forced upon us really. We had to make the best of a bad job, both of us. We had enough money to go round the corner to the pub down the road. It was next to the nurse's home, which was non-alcoholic. Trish had a gin and orange, and I had a beer. It completely put Trish off gin and orange. We never looked back.

One of my contemporaries was Michael O'Donnell[x]. He was one of the Cambridge Footlights people originally. He wrote a book about our group's expedition to Holland in the floods. He went on to become a journalist and was on the radio a lot. He ran all the Christmas Shows. Trish remembers his amazing wife, Catherine Dorrington Ward, who was an accomplished pianist. She was a medical student too and played at the St. Thomas' Christmas Shows which, in those days, were renowned for being absolutely 'the best'. There were two grand pianos in the students' bar - a big room - and Catherine played one piano and her brother came and played the other one. I was involved, as usual, behind the stage as a stage-hand cum manager. Putting on the shows was a very busy time and I do not know how we ever did any work. We still have the records made of them – old 78s - but no record player to play them on.

We got married in 1954. I was still a student. It was almost an illegal act to be married as a student, (as I think it was at Wye College), and married quarters were unheard of. We were that bit older, by that time, aged 24 and 25, and we had to make a decision because as soon as you were qualified, you went for a hospital house job. This was round the clock work. You were out of circulation all the time you were a houseman. So we reckoned that we would marry beforehand. Trish was qualified by then and had been doing midwifery. When you are qualified as a houseman, you cannot have your wife staying with you. This was left over from the pre-NHS days where it was a privilege if you got a house job in hospital and you more or less got paid as a doctor to work in a local hospital because it was there that you got your foothold into local practice. I always knew that I wanted to be in a country practice. I did not think of anything else really. When I was doing obstetrics I had felt that perhaps it might be a good idea to stay, but never got round to it.

My wedding to Trish (Patricia Flack - nee Boydell), 17th July 1954

We were married at Holy Trinity church, Brompton Road, London on17th July, 1954. We rented a flat in Kensington through a colleague. It was very much an attic flat where the servants would have been. The flat was on the fourth floor and had 67 stairs leading up to it. On the ground floor was a florist's shop; on the first floor lived Mr and Mrs Wells, the owners, and their son; on the second floor were a Portuguese psychiatric nurse, Julio, and his charge, a Portuguese son of a Portuguese noble; and we were in the attic. The roof leaked - we had a bucket on the dressing table - and mice in the kitchen which had escaped from the baker's next door. We later hung nappies on a string between chimney pots on the roof or in front of an electric fire. Nappies were boiled in a tub and prodded with a plunger. There was an old geyser for hot water.

Wedding group. Left to right: George Dixon, Kit Dixon, Me, Trish, Edith Boydell, Norman Boydell

Every day at 4.30pm Mrs Wells would waddle up the road to bank the day's takings. Times were hard and we had a standing arrangement that if she was short of cash, I would try to pay earlier. Trish earned £5 per week when qualified. My medical school grant just covered the rent and the money I inherited from my father was just enough to cover us until I qualified. I never failed an exam after I met Trish.

Mrs. Elizabeth Wells, landlady 1954

We said that we would not have any family for two and a half years - Trish's Father said, 'Well you two ought to know what you are talking about.' However, Caroline arrived a year after the day of our marriage. We were both horrified at first, quite frankly. But in fact Caroline was amazing and kept Trish company until I qualified a year later.

Trish only gave up work just before we had Caroline, and she went back afterwards, part time, working at the private Queensgate Clinic, which was just round the corner from where we lived. It specialised in obstetrics, gynaecology and urology. Trish used to leave the baby in her pram outside the flower shop on the pavement – she never thought twice about it. The florist's husband, who was in his 70s or 80s, and other residents, used to look after her if she was outside in the pram. The customers knew her – it was a different century.

It was a Greek Millionaire called Oscar Goulandris who gave us the pram. Trish had looked after his wife Olga for nine months at the Queensgate Clinic and he paid for a very upmarket pram as a 'thank you'.

I qualified in 1955. It was the day that President Craveiro Lopes of Portugal[xl] had come up the Thames in his naval cruiser called the Bartolomeu Dias. They went under Tower Bridge and were welcomed by the Queen. We had fired the salute in the morning and in the evening I went to find out whether I had passed or not. It was very interesting the way we found out whether we had passed or not. We met in a designated pub the evening before the results came out and a particular Professor would sit down and read out the names. I do not think that he should have done that.

I came home. When I arrived there was nobody in our flat but there was a lot of noise in the flat below where the Portuguese chap lived. So I went down and there were half a dozen sailors from the Bartolomeu Dias, Julio, Trish and our baby daughter who was being handed from sailor to sailor – and I announced: 'I am a Doctor!' They were already having a party, out of the blue. The sailors had left their ship with a bag of food and bottle of wine

I had got married. Post-qualifying you had to go and apply for residencies. My first job was in Maidstone at the West Kent Hospital[xii] in 1955, first Surgery, then Medicine. There was a very small number of us in the Hospital as residents - I think probably about six. Because there were so few of us we covered for each other, whether a chap was a House Physician or House Surgeon. There was a Registrar in the casualty department, a Registrar on the surgical department and that was about the lot. So if anybody was off, for the day or night, we covered for them and that was just normal - it was just expected. I do not remember any Contract or anything - this was just what you did. The hours one did were about 100 hours per week - it was just enormous. One did not expect anything different - it was totally normal. That was how you got experience. The Paediatrics came under Medicine and Surgery - there was no specialist paediatric service. One spent one's times with the kids too. The system was very good for training doctors - you saw everything, whether you liked it or not. Although I was doing Surgery, there was an Obstetrics unit there which was a GP unit: which means it was staffed by GPs; there was nobody resident for Obstetrics. There were Consultants for Obstetrics, but one lived in Chatham and the other, also in the Medway Towns, because there was a bigger unit in Chatham, and so if there were any problems that was where you had to send for them. In the meantime, the GPs were not always around, so, of course, we got involved. I never remember ever seeing any job description, it was just expected. Litigation was not there then.

The West Kent Hospital, Maidstone

One of the biggest regrets of my life was that I did not blow the whistle on one particular surgeon who did things that were totally out of order, and did not take responsibility. We had to find ways of avoiding him having any opportunity of doing anyone any harm and would refer people who came in to another Dr when we should not have done. We should have blown the whistle, but not just us, it was not the juniors that should have done it, it should have been more senior doctors who knew jolly well what was going on. We were in the position that if we complained, we would not get another job. You were entirely dependent on the good will you engendered with your bosses. That doctor was a General Surgeon and thought he was very clever with Orthopaedics, but had no idea at all. He was not old, but had a drink problem.

This doctor had funny ideas. One time he had the bright idea of taking a biopsy of somebody's rather swollen testes. So he made me go up to the ophthalmic hospital to get a thing called a 'little trephine' which you used to use for boring holes in eyes. His intention was to take a biopsy of this bloke's testes by making a small nick and pushing this thing in so that he could take the biopsy, which he did. Fine, but it went straight through a blood vessel and the testes swelled up so that it was like an enormous ball. Then the next week, this guy was at the end of the list for an orchiectomy (a removal of the testes). When it came to this particular patient, the surgeon upped sticks and told me to get on with it. Fortunately, the anaesthetist at the top end was a kindly man and talked me through the operation.

As a houseman we used to do simple things, like appendices. There was a great camaraderie between housemen because there had to be really to get on and cover for each other. So you never left anything undone. I was lucky because I did not have to apply for my next houseman's job; I was asked if I would do the Medicine job at the same hospital. I was six months doing the first job as a House Surgeon and six months in the second as a House Physician, although I think that it was a bit more than that as I overlapped with the next person. I only came home alternate weekends; Trish was in London with the baby. This justifies marrying when we did, because we knew that when I started house jobs, we would hardly see each other, so we were delighted to have a child actually. I only came home one weekend in two, and one half day a week. It was not worth coming for half a day a week, but I did occasionally. I would go home on Wednesday and go back at the crack of dawn on Thursday. We could not afford a car, so travel was by train.

All Saint's Hospital, Chatham

It so happened, that within the surgical post we spent one afternoon doing gynaecology because there was no gynaecological house surgeon. We worked with a chap called Stanley Wright, who actually must have got on with me because he later invited me to do his House job in All Saints Hospital, Chatham[xiii]. So the next thing was that I found myself in Chatham, after Maidstone. Chatham was a very mixed lot. It was an old hospital on top of a hill and it is the model for the Poor House Dickens wrote about in Oliver Twist. Part of the hospital had been built round the Poor House and there was still the room where Oliver Twist was supposed to have asked for more. This assignment was fortunate because there was a very experienced South African Registrar there who was an excellent teacher who allowed one to develop at maximum capacity; also senior doctors were always available. I almost decided to abandon the idea of general practice and specialise in Gynaecology obstetrics.

All Saint's Hospital, Chatham

This was 1956, the time of the Hungarian uprising, and there were a few Hungarian students who had managed to get out. The ones who were escaping were mostly students, because they were the ones who had been causing the riots in the uprising. They had been living in cellars and the like. They had flown into Manston, and then they were vetted. Some refugees among the patients from the Hungarian uprising had gynaecological problems, some were then found to have TB as well and they were put into an isolation unit in All Saints. As they were primarily gynaecology patients, despite the TB it was my job to look after them. I picked up TB then myself. I thought that I was just getting tired because of all the hard work and late nights. When I started as a houseman I used to be able to come back on duty after my weekend off and walk 'scouts pace' up the hill from the railway station to All Saints with no trouble at all. But as time went on I got slower and slower and in the end I just took a taxi. Then I realised that I had got trouble. Trish also realised that I had been coughing a lot, and I wasn't getting over it.

By chance, when I was at Maidstone they had got a new X-ray unit and I had been invited to have my picture taken. So when I had myself chest X-rayed in the Chatham hospital I said, 'Oh by the way, I had a chest X-ray at Maidstone,' and so I had a 'before and after' picture which showed the difference. So I obviously had not got TB when I was in Maidstone, but I caught it at All Saints. So I had to finish my full six months, I did five and a half. Dear Stanley

Wright signed me off for the full course, though, so I was able to take the Obstetrics exam. I did not need this to be a GP, but I enjoyed Obstetrics and Trish did Midwifery – so it was something special. Trish had been given a BCG vaccination when she was nursing, so she was protected against TB; all nurses had to have them. Interestingly I had not you see - Doctors did not have to.

I was referred to my own hospital, St Thomas'. I did not have it badly - one patch in my left lung. At my own hospital I saw a very flamboyant consultant who waved his arms about and said 'Oh yes, no problem at all – we treat you on the hoof these days'. My father had had TB and had spent years in convalescent homes and I was thinking that that might happen, but this man was so enthusiastic that I can see him now writing the prescription out and saying 'We believe in multiple therapy these days – streptomycin (by injection) and pills - para-aminosalicylate sodium (PAS) and INAH, the lot – take this'. So I went off to the Pharmacy, had to wait ages and was then given an enormous bag of stuff for three months. In it was a box with a syringe - I had to have streptomycin every day which Trish was to give me, being a nurse. She had to give it to me every day. She used an old-fashioned syringe made of metal with huge needles – I was terrified of needles - into my buttock, once a day in the morning. And I had to take 27 pills and granules per day - eight pills three times and three once a day. I was not a happy lad at all. I think that this was one of the lowest times of my life really. I had eight pills - three times a day and one three times a day and then there was this injection, so this was the treatment. Trish had to give me the injection before I got up. That was fine, but on the tenth day I started falling over and I felt queasy and sick like the day after having had too much to drink the night before. We got a chap out but not the flamboyant doctor. When you got hold of the hospital they had a system for students and this chap with blue suede shoes came out – he was the doctor. He came all the way upstairs and was very churlish about the accommodation we were in – he was one of the Chelsea doctors. I was taken into hospital and of course I'd had a reaction to the streptomycin which knocked out my sense of balance. Trish remembered that I went into hospital and they poured ice cold water into my eardrum to see if I would react. I didn't and it was Trish who realised that my nerves had been damaged by the streptomycin, which can occur. That is why right through general practice and even now, I have always had to say to patients, 'Please leave your light on along the path so that I can find my way up to your door at night.' I always went with a torch. I worried more about that than my TB quite honestly – TB was curable, but my balance was not – it was for life. I went off this flamboyant doctor.

Trish's father in Eastbourne saw me pushing the pram and said, 'Right, Gerald, you had better learn golf – that will get you walking'. So I was carted off to the golf course, which was just below the house, and I stood there with my legs apart with the ball in front and Pa-in-Law telling me how to strike it on the tee. I took one swipe at the ball and fell flat on my face. I could only walk, literally, holding onto the pushchair. Eventually I went to see an ENT (Ear, Nose and Throat) person of some renown, who was not exactly helpful and said of my balance 'Oh well, that is it. You are probably going to have this for the rest of your life. You will not recover. You are going to have to cope with it and plan your life. One thing that you will not be able to do is go into general practice', which was not a very helpful thing to say. He said, 'You know, you are going to have trouble in the dark.'

While at All Saint's Hospital, Chatham with Caroline, 23 months

I realized that the only thing to do was exercise and went out on the golf course, did daylight walking and became reasonably fit. Unfortunately, I overdid it and at a follow up examination, my lung lesion had grown and I was put into hospital for a month. I was put in a side ward and barrier-nursed. I said that I would discharge myself, so instead they stuck me on a balcony in a ward facing the Houses of Parliament!

During the course of my illness, Trish produced our second child, Marianne, and I took my Obstetrics diploma and passed that. That was an interesting thing, I went to Hackney Hospital for the viva examination. There was an option of taking either a lift or stairs, and as it said 'lift for the elderly or disabled', I went up the stairs, and by the time I got up to the top, I was knackered. Fortunately, the exam was very easy because Marianne had been born in a strange way – face first, which is a bit unusual. So I sat down with the examiners and the first thing they said was, 'Can you tell us what you know about face presentation?' So I said, 'You will not believe this, Sirs, but only last week...... and they spent their time congratulating me and asking me what my family did – so that was fun and there was a bit of luck!

It was at this stage that we were seriously thinking, actually quite determined, to go to Vancouver. There were not many jobs going in this country then, or not the sort that we wanted. We already had friends who had gone out there and I had actually got a place at the Shaughnessy Hospital, Vancouver - we were planning to go when I finished the house jobs; .but that was before I got TB. The Canadians would not touch me with a barge pole. The authorities said that I could not enter British Columbia until I had had a clear X-ray for five years, so we could not go. Then the most important thing was for me to walk on my own, without any aid – it was like being a child learning to walk. It was all right pushing a pram. We were still living in the flat above the florist in London, but with two children.

Throughout my house jobs I had gone through the National Health Service. But even in the hospitals, there was still a left-over from the pre-NHS days because I do not ever remember signing any bit of paper, contract, or agreement as a houseman; you just got the job and were very glad to get it. In fact, the number of resident housemen was very small but one's experience was enormous because of covering for each other. So when one was a house physician, one still did surgery, casualty and the odd anaesthetics, because there was nobody else there to do it. Nowadays there are very strong lines of demarcation: you cannot do more than 46 hours and if you are a house surgeon you do not stand in for anybody else as that is in your contract. It was a totally different world. It meant though, that maybe the patients suffered, but we had an incredible experience of everything. It was good training; one had seen most things before one went into practice, which was a big advantage. My pay was £250 per annum less £150 for residency.

It was traditional in the country that if you got a house job it was a privilege and I am not too sure that you got paid pre-NHS. It was expected of you to carry on in the pre-NHS way, which was that you were there and you worked your 100 hours per week and were totally involved, because you were anticipating that if you did all right you might get a job in the area. It was the same as being an 'intern' today. I really did think that way because when I was in Maidstone, I thought that I might get a job around Maidstone. I got to know the GPs and vice-versa, because you referred patients back to them and they referred them to you and we got to know them through meetings. However, that all came adrift when I was not available any more when I was ill.

CHAPTER 6: JOINING THE WYE PRACTICE AS A TRAINEE 1958

I applied for posts in London to start with. I used to go to BMA House and they would give you a list of openings. Trish recalled that I went for an interview at Wood Green and was seen by this chap who offered the job and said to me – 'Vil you do all zee night calls?' I said, 'I am sorry, but I have a balance problem.' So I did not go to Wood Green.

It was a strange time. The poor old GPs were very badly paid, and they could not afford to take on assistants unless they were trainees, because they got paid for a trainee for one year. So if you were a trainee, you were a trainee for a year and that was the end of it. It was a hard time, because the Principals were paid per capita so your entire income was totally dependent on the number of patients you had. As patients were slow to come forward to register, which they usually left until they needed a doctor urgently, there was little love lost between GPs, who often poached patients from each other.

I had always wanted a practice in the country and in Kent. Both our families were in Kent and Sussex. Also I had got a Kent Grant and felt I really wanted to put something back. So when I heard of an opening at Wye, I applied.

I was given an appointment at Wye and came down here. I was met at the station by the daughter of the practice, Marion, and then met the principal doctor, who was a lady, Dr Ana Balfour, and her husband, Mac, who was the

The Doctor's House in Upper Bridge Street, Wye

partner who took me round the practice in Ana's Vauxhall Victor. Mac took me round the surgery which, in later years, became a solicitor's office. It was certainly the Dr Finlay era. It was absolutely what I had expected of a rural practice: a waiting room, a consulting room, and a "sluice" with bottles of medicines. No loo. It was on the opposite side of the road to their house, which had been the Doctor's house for years and years. Later it became the Wife of Bath restaurant.

Top: The Old Surgery, Upper Bridge Street

Above: Drs. Ana and Mac Balfour

Having been round the surgery, before lunch in their home, Mac said to me 'Would you like to join us at the practice?' and I said 'Well I would, but I ought to tell you that I have got a balance problem'. We were all three in what is now the dining room in the Wife of Bath, and Ana was sitting, as she always sat, with one leg on a foot rest and a rug round her. She said, 'Well, what is your problem?' I explained that my problem was with my balance and might hinder my ability to make visits at night. Her response was to take her rug off and there was her one leg and her calliper beside it. I did not know she only had one leg when I came. She said 'What's your problem!'

I had seen my trainee predecessor, who was obviously not happy with the practice. He told me everything possible to put me off taking the job and I thought, this cannot be right. Nobody is as bad as that. He was lying there with a bad back. He said, 'I have been put upon,' and this, that and the other. 'I have been called out at night.' He obviously thought the traineeship was a sinecure and he should do the minimum. My ideas were totally different - the more, the merrier. So I had been offered the job and took it.

Trish believed we were to receive £750 per year plus £150 car allowance. I think that the figure was less than that and included £150 for covering two weekends in three. We had a flat owned by the practice – the upstairs of Fern Villa 1905, 116 Bridge Street, which was opposite the George pub. The Balfours had bought it and turned it into two flats. We started at the top. Frank and Ann Taylor were below us and had been there for some time before we came. We lived there for a long time, and then we eventually bought the whole house.

Trish had to be vetted and was invited to lunch on a separate occasion. She recalled sitting down in their dining room being waited on by a maid at a vast table with Mac and Ana at each end and Mac carving a joint on the dresser as a flock of noisy sheep was being driven down Bridge Street. This was her introduction to Wye.

Top: Fern Villas, Bridge Street

Above: The George Pub, Bridge Street

In order to get the job I had to buy a car. It cost me £250 – a black Ford Prefect – the one that looked like a Lada. I bought it in London from a pal of my dear uncle. It was some odd place we bought it from, underneath a railway arch, and I had not driven for a long time – not since I had been in the army – so it was a bit dodgy. We drove down to Kent in it. When I had been a medical student I had a Lea Francis - a 1926 model - which I bought specially for our honeymoon. It was a beautiful car. It broke down in Battersea eventually and never went any further.

We moved to Wye on 28 February, 1958. There was snow and ice and poor weather - the coldest night we had ever had. The road was blocked at Lenham and our removals van arrived too late to fit us into the flat, so we had to spend the first night in the Balfours' house, with Caroline aged three and a half and Marianne, the baby, in a carrycot. Perhaps Caroline was in a bed with us, I cannot remember. It was bitterly cold and the wind was blowing, but we could not shut the window. It was a sash window in the front of the house. There was a big gap at the top and the wind came straight down Church Street, round the corner and into our bed. Mac was a Scot. The bed was one of these musical beds, with two hair mattresses on it. It was solid, but had a dip in the middle and we had a terrible night, never to be forgotten.

In the morning, I took the car out and scratched the whole side on the wall that was sticking out. They have chopped off the end now. I went straight to Taylor's Garage. They said, 'Not another one!' This was my first visit to Taylor's Garage. So it was not a very good start. On March 1st I was marched straight into work. Poor old Trish had to go home because the removal men had eventually arrived. She had to sort out all that. In the flat, not a plug fitted the sockets. We had brought the wrong plugs which were three-pin round fitments, and whatever they had was different from what we had brought. Fortunately, there was an electrician in the village then - Rex (the flex) Rumley and he had plugs, so we were all right. (His father "Whip" was the carter for Denne's Mill.)

When I really realised that I was in the right place was, I think, when the Balfours went on holiday in early April that year. They were going away and had a lady locum who lived a long way away, about 15 miles I think, to cover me, because it was the law that a trainee should not be on his own. I was given a list of things to do and people to see whilst they were away. These were the routine visits to the aged in case they died - as you could only sign their death certificates if you had seen them in the previous fortnight - and a list of the chronically sick, a lot of whom were the regulars, i.e. the 'A' list – ('private but not private'), that were routine visits, who I did not normally see. Then there were the baby clinics and injections to do etc. At the very end of the list it said, 'Please would you open the garage doors because the swallows will be arriving.' (Mac always had a big sheet over his open Morris Minor to keep off the swallows' messes.) It was the very last thing that Mac had written down. 'Yes,' I thought, 'this must be the right practice!'

Then Granny Forge, (who at one time lived in the middle of Hastingleigh Woods), used to come and look after the house. She would take messages if necessary as the phone was connected through to us permanently, apart from when it was put through to Taylor's Garage. It was generally expected, that the wife was part of the practice, very much so. Knowing that Trish was a nurse, and knowing that She had two children, gave people a lot of reassurance. It was a tremendous help to me that I had (a) a wife and (b) children.

CHAPTER 7: BACKGROUND TO THE WYE PRACTICE

Before it was the Balfours' practice, local memories were mostly about a Dr Sharples. I have this list from the Wye Historical archives of the doctors in Wye and their dates from about 17th century.

WYE MEDICAL PRACTITIONERS

Year	Surname	Name / Address	Occupation
1624	Richman	Ambrose *(d.5.5.1642)*	Medical Doctor Chaplin *(7.4.24)* Curate of Wye *(1.10.1627)*
1774	Scudamore	William	Doctor Apothecary
1841	Morris	William *(b.1816)* 114 Bridge Street	Apothecary
from 1845			Surgeon
1845	Wildash	John	Surgeon
1862	Brook	William Frederick	Surgeon
1874	Manning	Joseph	Surgeon
from 1891			Surgeon, Medical Officer
1905	Sills	Clarence Ham Field View House Bridge Street	Physician Surgeon, Medical Officer Public Vaccinator
1915	Sharples	Joseph Percival 4 Upper Bridge Street	Physician Surgeon
from 1930			Doctor
1935	Murray-Jones	4 Upper Bridge Street	Physician & Surgeon
from 1946			Surgery
1946-	Balfour	Ana	Doctor
1964	Balfour	McDonald	Doctor

Dr. Sharples is the doctor that I am acquainted with in so far as the very old patients remembered him when they were children. He lived in the Doctor's house at 4 Upper Bridge Street, i.e. the Wife of Bath. He rode a horse – there were stables behind the house, and there was a Mr and Mrs Jordan - I think he was his 'ostler' who looked after the horses. A Mr and Mrs Jordan were still about when we arrived at Wye, but they were the next generation. Dr. Sharples was renowned for enjoying the good life, because nearly all the people who talked about him said 'Yes, they knew that about him when they were younger'. One particular lady remembered him because she was in service at the Wye Aerodrome, which was behind the station in the First World War, and she told me that he would be down there most days in the Officers' Mess and he would be taken home in a cart. I do not know whether that was an exaggeration. Also other ladies told me that he was very good when women were in labour, but was not so good when he left them because, obviously, he was 'well looked after'. He used to arrive on horseback, but on leaving, he got on one side of the horse and fell off the other.

Dr Sharples was succeeded by a chap called Dr Murray-Jones. I do not know much about him except I believe he was a good cricketer. At that time, medicine was all either private, and paid for, or it was what you called the 'Lloyd George' Scheme[xiv]. This is complicated, but there were cards called 'Lloyd George cards' which some people paid into at so much per week. So they did not have to keep the money in the teapot, or whatever. I think it was probably a sort of forerunner of national insurance cards. I do know that Dr Murray-Jones also lived in the Doctor's house and I did meet his wife. I am not sure whether he died and the practice became vacant. A patient recalls that he had a monkey that kept escaping.

When the Balfours came they must have taken over the practice prior to the start of the National Health Scheme in 1948, since they bought it from Dr Murray Jones. Ana Balfour was a Dutch American who qualified in Edinburgh. They had their two children before the war and, because of her American nationality, Ana was able to go to America for the war. She went off to Maine, taking the children, and was in practice there. Mac Balfour stayed behind, because at that time, they had a practice, I believe, in Cowes on the Isle of Wight, and he was there throughout the war. I do not think that he had a very good war because it was obviously a place of a lot of action. I think that he had a difficult time.

When Ana came back from America they then bought the Wye practice, which is what one did then. Ana was the senior partner because Mac decided that he would try to study for a higher degree to become a consultant. He tried to get a

Membership of the Royal College of Physicians. It was a difficult time for him because there were a lot of young people coming out of the forces de-mobbed, and he'd had a hard time in his Cowes practice. Unfortunately, he did not get his exams, he had just wanted to specialise in medicine. Therefore he was always the junior partner, Ana was the senior partner, it was her practice. I do not know how much she bought the practice for. In those days you bought the 'goodwill' of the surgery. As Mac had unfortunately failed his exams, financially it was a terrible situation to be in at the time. The health service had not started then and they depended on private patients or the Lloyd George Scheme.

In 1948 the National Health Service started so they became part of the health scheme and were dependent then on a patient head count. You did not actually get paid until patients joined you. I think that you did inherit all the existing patients who were on the list of the Lloyd George Scheme. The National Health Service had been strongly resisted between 1946 and 1948 by doctors. The BMA resisted it all the way along. During the war (1942) Beveridge[xv] wrote his watershed report on social security, which essentially said the country needed a health service. Nye Bevan[xvi] in the post-war Labour Party then introduced the NHS Act in 1946, which was fantastic. But the great barrier was that he could not get the BMA to budge. Eventually he managed to get them to do so, saying 'I stuffed their mouths with gold'. What he did was not only to allow them to be paid by the NHS but also to have private patients. They had 'elevenths'. Two elevenths were allowed for private patients and nine elevenths were to be within the health scheme. Now – which of those two elevenths they made available for private patients was up to them, and very often one suspected that it was the other way around. The consultants could not be monitored. Trish recalled that it very often caused real division, because they had to travel away from the NHS hospital, as they do now, to see their private patients. Where it worked best was in the teaching hospitals in London where they had a private wing. So if you needed a consultant urgently on an NHS ward, they were just around the corner in the same hospital. But when GPs outside were looking for a consultant, saying 'where is so and so', we were told 'He is at St. ....' You could never get the guy because he was at 'St. Elsewhere's'.

The BMA was then dominated totally by the consultants; GPs were very much second-class citizens, and totally dependent on them. Mind you, the consultants were also dependent on GPs to refer patients – but it was they who ran the BMA. Once Nye Bevan had got them on side, the rest followed, but the GPs had a very difficult time when their practice was bought from them by the NHS because they could not get the money until they retired. It was put on one side until then, so presumably they were locked into their practice until they were 60.

Dorothy Coulter

As Ana had one leg, she was not very mobile; she was very much the more dominant of the pair. Because of her immobility, there was a lot of very loud shouting going on in order for her not to have to move. When Mac failed his degree to become a consultant, he joined Ana as a partner. Mind you, Mac did all the work and Ana did the administration. During the time when she had been on her own at the practice, it produced quite a few problems. There were people who found having a lady doctor, and perhaps a one-legged lady doctor, difficult. One got the message that she did not have an easy time with everybody. When Mac joined, he changed the situation somewhat and people who had left, came back. Around Wye at that time there were few lady doctors, there was a lady in Lenham. As time went on there were more and more.

Mac being more mobile than Ana, and with his GP experience, did most of the medicine. From 1950 onwards, they had a series of annual trainees, which was allowed. I think that they had six before me. It was very interesting when I first came, because the patients would tell me that they remembered them all and there were some that they liked and some not. They wished that the trainee who was two before me had stayed, as he had fitted in. The next chap did not, which was to my advantage, of course. I gathered that the patients were fed up with a different doctor every year. The trainee was expected to do a fair amount of the work and I think the feeling got back that patients felt that they'd had enough of this. I did not know this until later on when people told me. I think that people had put their oar in. Perhaps that is why later they asked me to stay.

When we arrived in Wye, Marion Balfour was 20 and David was 18, so we were nearer their age group than their parents' age group. David spent a lot of time with us – escaping I think, as one does when one is a teenager. Marion, to her horror, was sent away to boarding school and lost contact locally. She did know Dorothy Coulter well and the other person was Mrs Curtis, who was a dressmaker. Marianne was later a bridesmaid to Marion and Mrs Curtis made the bridesmaids' dresses.

Ana had a lot of stories about how she managed to get around in the snow and ice. A carpet was put across the road from their house at the Wife of Bath to the surgery on the opposite side of the road when it snowed, and then she would hop across. She was once put in a wheelbarrow to get to Marriage Farm for a birth; it had been the only way to get her there. I also heard the story about a youngster who had lost an arm. He had been playing with a Mills bomb or something that he had found on the Downs and somehow she had managed to get up to him on the Downs to look after him. How, I do not know. She kept going. There were no staff involved at all at the surgery, the only staff were domestic staff. The Balfours still had Mr and Mrs Jordan Jnr. Mrs Jordan helped in the house, she was their housekeeper. Mr Jordan, whose father had been ostler to Murray-Jones, had succeeded him, later becoming chauffeur. Mrs Betts also used to help in the house. As far as the practice was concerned, there were no secretarial staff. Everything we did, we did ourselves.

Budgen's Store in Church Street

Ana was renowned for having a very loud horn in her car. Whether or not she had had the volume specially increased, I do not know. Everyone knew when she was about. She sounded her horn outside Bugdens, the grocer, and out they would come with her order. The same with Maxted the butcher and dear Dorothy Coulter would come leaping out from Geerings the newsagent with the papers. I would not be surprised to find she also had an arrangement with the bank. She had a very strong personality and a notorious voice that could rouse Mac from the garden. He did a lot of gardening as far away as he could! She did not have an American accent - she had lost it. She entertained a lot with the 'great and the good'. In 1946 there was obviously a social set in the village, a separate social set of the 'establishment' from around and about.

Ana was a socialite and she was very good at entertaining. She was very well read and had a lot of interests. In consequence, I think a lot of people joined the practice and when Mac came, they increased. I did sit down once and wrote down the number of colonels and majors etc. registered with the practice. There was a very large number, and of course Dunstan Skilbeck, Principal of Wye College. The College was very important to them because there were 400 students and they all registered with the practice. They also always forgot to de-register when they left which meant that there were quite a few on their list who should not have been.

Mac always had a dog, a black labrador called Tammy – after Tam O' Shanter, I presume. Mac had a little Morris Minor convertible, cream with a maroonish top and I think it has come back into the village. I think that Etienne, the

French Conjuror, owns it now. You would have thought that there were two people in the car because the dog would sit up in the passenger seat and as the car was going away you could see Mac's head with the cap on and the dog's ears beside him. The dog would nip out of the car from time to time and not come back. He was 'entire' and obviously knew all the ladies around. If Mac got a call and the dog had left the car, of course he had to go, and had to leave the dog somewhere. More than a couple of times, I was going out on my rounds and I would see this foot-sore dog on the way home. He just jumped in my car and I would take him back and found poor old Mac had gone all over the place looking for him. He was a lovely dog. We had hardly been in the practice when the dog got knocked down and broke its leg and I was left in charge of the practice when the dog and the family went up to the vets. Sadly, they weren't able to take him when they moved to France.

The Balfours retired in 1964. They were not going to retire then, but to my surprise they suddenly decided that they'd had enough. Ana was possibly two years older than Mac. She had been in the health scheme from the very beginning – from 1948 to 1964 - and she had reached retirement age. I presume that when she came to retirement age, the money that had been kept on one side for her, which had been the "goodwill" bought by the NHS, could be released. There was then, officially, no more "goodwill" in a practice after 1948. That went because the State had bought the "goodwill" from all the GPs that year, so when I joined as a partner, I did not have to pay "goodwill". It was illegal for an NHS practice to sell goodwill after 1948 because of this.

When she retired, I presume that they then got the lump sum and worked it out that they could afford to retire to France. They had a little place in France and had been going there for years. They were popular there, and had made friends for life. There was a tale of Ana going to fetch a parcel from the post office there. The parcel was a new boot for her – it was a left one. The chap behind the counter at the post office, seeing what it was, said 'oh perhaps we could come to some arrangement, Madame. I have lost my other leg'! The climate suited her because of her rheumatoid arthritis. We holidayed there a couple of times and visited them, although we did not actually stay with them. Mac would walk for miles in France while Ana still continued to drop him off and pick him up.

CHAPTER 8: TRAINEE GP AT WYE

The Health Scheme *(National Health Service)* began in 1948. I have an idea that the Lloyd George Scheme went automatically then. As said, when the Balfours had the practice, there was very little income because the capitation fees were based on a patient 'head count'. You did not get a capitation fee until someone came and said 'I want to join you' and registered. Patient numbers had dropped after the war, when Ana was the main doctor, as some patients had left the practice put off by her being a lady. Also, sometimes when doctors came from Ashford to cover, they poached patients. But when Mac joined after being away studying they all came back slowly. The private patients who lived all over the place, bided their time and did not bother to register until they went ill, so it was a very hard time for the Balfours to be in the practice then.

We came to Wye, when the NHS was established. For a GP practice, the Wye finances were very complicated. There was a capitation fee, and there were also dispensing fees payable. In a rural practice you also got a mileage fee and there was also something called 'difficulty of access', for places like Marriage Farm, for example. It was called 'walking units' where you could not get your car near to the house. I used to take my children with me to open gates etc. Finance was all very confusing.

At this time in a rural area, ownership of cars was a luxury, also there were not many families with phones up in the hills – it was very much an outdoor practice. The State agreement with GP practices was that you were responsible for the people registered with you for 365 days per year. Although GPs were allowed any number of private patients, people thought that the NHS free care was a good idea, and very few of the former private patients bothered to continue as private. It was the same doctor that they saw so why pay? However, there was sort of a two tier system which I found difficult to understand. The old private patients, even when under the NHS, seemed to think that they ought to be treated as private. They felt that they had rights because of their 'standing'. I found this very difficult.

I do not think that there was any special training about becoming a GP and building up relationships, I cannot remember anything; I think that one learnt it from Mac and Ana, their relationships and how to handle them and so on. Mind you, you could be unlucky and be attached to a practice that was terrible. I had apprehensions because having been told I could not cope with general practice because of my balance, I wondered whether or not I could. But then being reassured by Ana that I could ('what's your problem?'), I felt better. I learnt the hard way, very much so.

I explained earlier that, as a result of the treatment that I had received for TB, I worried about my ability to keep my balance, particularly on night visits. I remember that one of my first visits at night was to Glebe House, which is in Boughton Aluph, the house next door to Boughton Aluph Church; not the absolute next door, but it has a long drive through overhanging trees. I got called there, not knowing where it was, so I had to search for it. The instructions were always pretty poor: 'you know where it is – by the church.' One gets to know churches and pubs and phone boxes as the most important things to remember. I went on this visit and parked outside, not realising that the curved drive was 100 yards long. I could see a light through the trees and followed my way in by the light. I used to say to people, 'leave a light on' so that I could see where I was going and because of my balance. Provided that I could see, I was all right. I got to the house, made the visit. It was a very strange visit because they were obviously colonials. The place was like a hot house with tropical flowers and peacock chairs and I thought that in the middle of Kent this was very odd. All the furniture was oriental. I said, 'do you mind leaving the light on when I go'. The husband had called me out on behalf of his wife, and was very gruff and fed up, obviously he was not at all happy. I had hardly got out of the door when he put the light off. It was sheeting with rain, totally dark, and I kept on falling over and, in the end, crawled out on my hands and knees for the last part. I got in the car and all I could do was laugh. I went home and told Trish and she thought it was funny too. Trish and I knew the people who lived there later on. She was Dorothy Eustace, a GP and one of the Percy family - quite an original person coming from Northumberland.

We prescribed at the practice, which I personally, when I started, did not like at all. I liked somebody between me and my patients' medicines, a proper pharmacist for this. We were prescribing from the boot of the car and in the surgery we had stock bottles and we made up the medicines ourselves. Most of the prescribing was liquid. The only pills we had were barbiturates to calm everybody down, antibiotics M&B *(May & Baker's Sulphapyridine)*, acromycin, chloromycetin (which was banned in the end), penicillin, digitalis folia, which as one knows, is just the leaf of a foxglove. That was a greeny tablet which was just a compressed powder. And then there were a whole series of 12oz bottles of this, that and the other which we made from concentrate and then diluted with tap water. We put our own labels on the bottles. You did carry a lot of made-up medicines and pills in the back of your car, and in the early years, we had to collect sixpence per prescription, which I hated. My pockets were full of sixpences.

Things were pretty limited. I suppose one had read books about rural practice and it was just as I had expected that it would be. A very tiny surgery, with a truckle bed with the legs cut off for Ana, who could not stand up to examine people, she had to sit down to do this. So the rest of us, Mac and I, knelt. The area that we covered was quite restricted at first. It included Wye, Hastingleigh, Brook, Godmersham, Crundale, Waltham, hardly into Brabourne and hardly over the level crossing, although Boughton Aluph was included. We had other patients dotted about who, historically I think, had been private patients under the old scheme. In the current Wye surgery there was a map which Dr Mac drew for me, showing me how to get around the practice. He had marked on it the names from the practice where there were people 'of note' whom he used to visit. There was the Reverend Champion, who was vicar of Chilham, and Colonel this, and Colonel that, and Dolly Archer, who was a regular twice or three times a week. I owned the map and left it on the wall in the surgery when I retired, but I now have it back. You could see it on the wall going down to the consulting rooms. Mac was really a first class doctor. He was excellent and I learnt an awful lot from him. The Balfours got funded for having me and I got paid by them.

The Practice did not have a nurse then. There were District Nurses, who were employed by the County. They were geographically located, one in Wye and one in Chilham. We were lucky, actually, because then there was a nurse/midwife qualification which no longer exists, and because there was not enough midwifery to cover their time completely they did practical nursing as well – District Nursing as well as District Midwifery. They were quite special.

In the practice, we had no staff; we did all our own letters – in longhand. Mac had the most immaculate writing and was a really excellent note-taker. Ana's was difficult, mine was worse. Trish remembered that we had a meeting with Mac in their house every morning with Ana telling her husband and me where we were to go to visit. She organised it because she took all the phone calls in the morning. It was not just phone calls because a lot of people did not have phones when we first started and there would be notes through the door – 'please would you come to see ......' Ana did the morning surgeries, so the word amongst patients was: 'if you want certificates and prescriptions, go in the mornings, but if you want your shirt off, go in the evenings!'

When Trish was not at home to take calls then the phone was put through to Taylor's Garage. They were wonderful in Taylor's Garage because telephones were at a premium and one had a list to give to them when one went out on one's rounds - usually two rounds, one early, whilst Ana was taking the messages and doing the morning surgery. Only one person could take the surgery because there was only one room. So she did the mornings in general; she took all the messages and saw all the people in the morning. It was a bit of a joke that

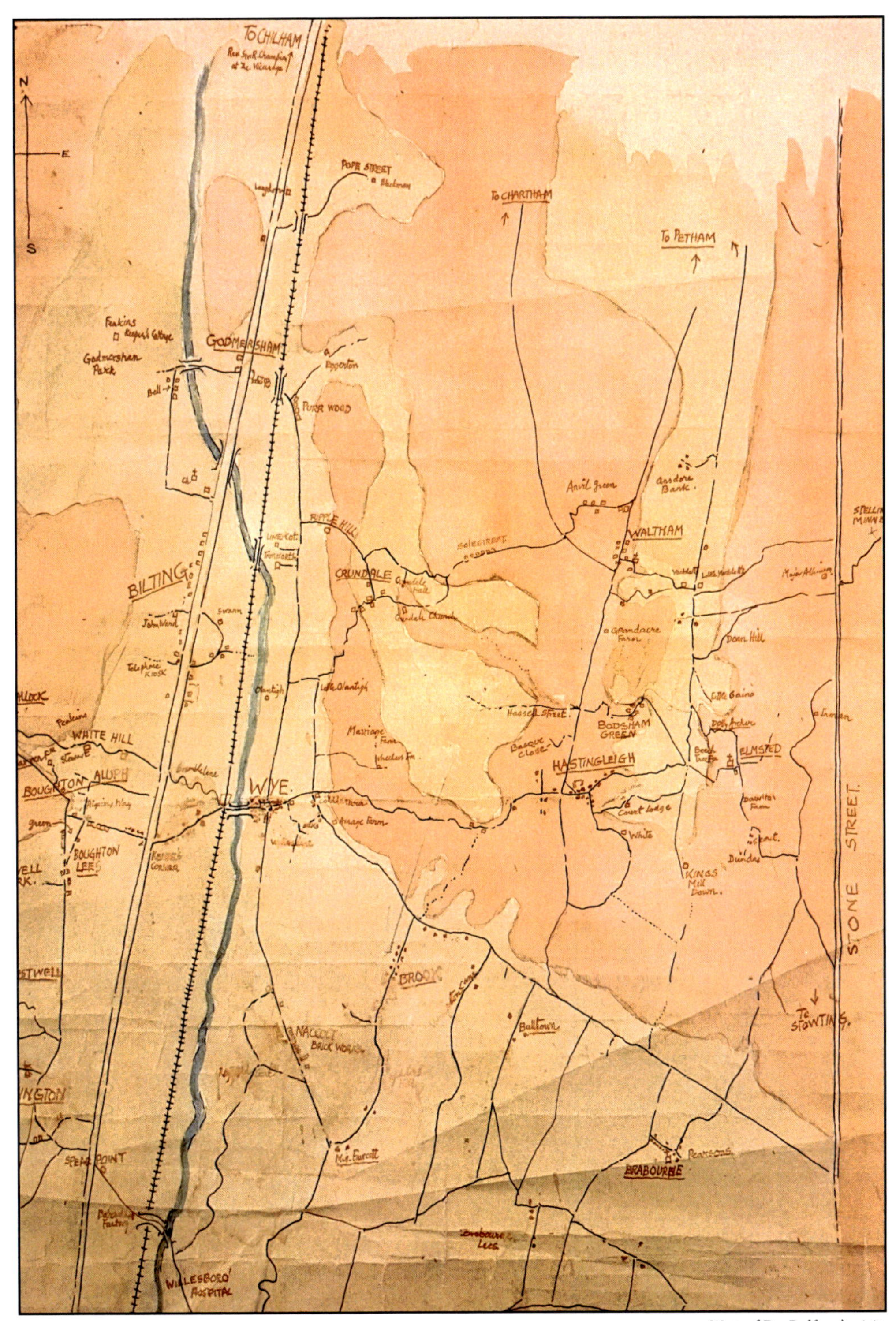

Map of Dr. Balfour's visits

people did not take their clothes off in the morning. It took too long to get them off and on when she was taking phone calls as well, so she was not enthusiastic about it. They had to come back in the evening. Patients would say to me in the evening, 'Oh I saw Dr Ana this morning,' and I would say 'Ah, and you have come again!' Every day we gave Taylors Garage a list of where we were going, and the names of all the people, putting against them OT or NOT (on telephone or not on telephone). If there was a real emergency they would go and find us.

Taylors Garage

They had two notice boards, one for the Doctor, and one for the mechanics. There was once the following message on the Doctor's notice board, 'Please fit two brass nipples for Miss Graham'. It was not really a mix up at all; it was their sense of humour. It then read on after, 'to lawnmower!' Brian Lepper ran Taylor's Garage at that time, he was the brother who died. Sid was always milling about; he ran the operations and sold the cars. Brian was more in the office. Communication was difficult then, but on the other hand, the arrangement worked.

An average day was that we used to have visits left over from the day before. This was routine, because one did a lot of visiting to people who had not got transport, so it was outside the village visiting, and one would visit frequently. It was a good way of getting to know people. If you saw them with their chest infection at home, you would say, 'I will come back the day after tomorrow,' and you would see them in the morning. They would then be in your diary. You would make the follow -up visits before going in to Ana at 11.00 am to get a new list, unless there were some urgent things left over from the night. During the day the phone usually went to the garage who took over from Ana but, at the end of the day, it was put through to Trish, or across the road if I was doing the surgery, and I then had to put it through to home. The switchboard was in the Doctor's House, (where the Wife of Bath bar was). One extension went across the road to the surgery, one went upstairs to the Balfours' bedroom, one went to the garage and one went to us. It was just a single line. When Ana rang through, it was not, 'Could you ask Gerry to go to so and so?' It was, 'Patricia! tell Gerald to go and see ....' But she was very funny because if it was a question of going to see, for example, someone at Godmersham Park, then Mac was there like a shot. It was a two-tier system in the practice, very much so. Mac went to the front door and I went to the back door, as it were, but of course, it was all very odd because, in theory, as a trainee in the first year one should not have been left on one's own to do anything. One was being supervised all the time. But I suppose one did not want to be supervised and wanted to get on and so one just got on with it. I was keen to see if I could cope and so it was exactly the practice that I had wanted, and I just felt at home, straight away. I felt that this was right but Trish, coming from London, felt that it was strange. She was a 'townie'. We had two children when we came, Caroline and Marianne; Johnny and William were born in 1960 and 1964.

The practice differed from today because transport was a big thing. As time went on I was not doing as many house visits because more people would come to the Surgery. It was convenient for them to do so rather than wait in for you. If you were expecting a visit from the doctor, you would ring up in the morning at 7.00 am or so and if it was Waltham, for example, I would not get there until perhaps 3 o'clock in the afternoon. I noticed in my diary that I had done 30 visits per day in a 'flu epidemic because I was going back to see the same patients the next day and numbers really multiplied.

We had an au pair then and Trish used to come out with me to help look after some patients when things got busy, and to keep me company in case I got stuck in a snow drift. We started early in the morning and went on late at night. We would come home, have supper and then go out and do more visits. In 1958 polio vaccination came in and the Balfours were on holiday. There had been a serious epidemic nearby in Maidstone, so it was important that children were protected. Trish put up notices in the villages for children to come to clinics for this. There were all these kids and no nurse. Trish was put in charge and all bar two had the injections. These two ran away. We rang the parent up and went out to inject them at night in their beds. It was a desperate thing to do, but their mum agreed. This illustrates how Trish, as nurse and wife, was very involved in the practice of a rural GP.

CHAPTER 9: END OF TRAINEESHIP

At the end of my time as a trainee, the Balfours said that they were not thinking of retiring, but they were thinking ahead in so many years time. They had the greatest difficulty in arranging for me to stay on because the responsible NHS County Executive, at Maidstone, said that there were enough doctors in the area. The area in the countryside extended down to places like Sevington, Brabourne, Aldington, Mersham, and there were enough doctors in the area covering it and they were not going to put any more in there. But they said 'yes you can, if he becomes a partner', which I could not understand. I think that they had to make me a partner in order for me to stay, but I became a fixed salary partner as it were.

The winter of 1962/63 was when there was a very, very long period of snow and ice. During this winter, we also had another terrible 'flu epidemic so one would visit patients daily because they needed seeing. At the same time as the bad 'flu epidemic, all the children who went to Bodsham School, as well as many under school age, who had escaped measles for years, got it, and it was very busy. Taylors (the garage) were very good. They would do anything and would provide a Landrover if necessary. I got up the hills using heavy-duty tyres which were soft rubber, which you could still use without chains. Then if there was a disaster, I did have a set of chains. We were well equipped. If I went up the hill, I tried to take someone with me with a shovel - often Trish came once we had au pairs. We had au pairs because we found that it was essential for us to have flexibility. I did a lot of my visits at night that bad winter. It was the best time because you could see somebody coming; but the snow ploughs were out everywhere which were a great help. The roads were like glass. It was a most extraordinary time. There was no treatment of roads then. Getting up to Hastingleigh and to such as Dolly Archer in Elmstead was quite a feat.

Wye in the snow

Visiting someone at home instead of seeing them at the surgery was tremendously informative. Knowing them at home, and probably meeting the rest of their family as well, it was always very easy to pick up where one left off with a patient as you had an association already. You could say

'How's Charlie?' you know, to show you knew something about them. It was what I called, 'Family Medicine' – that was the best way of describing it. You were treating the family; you were not just treating one patient.

If people needed referring to a specialist, Mac had a lot of London connections. I did not have any London connections, really, so used the local consultants; you could select the consultant to the patient, as it were, because some consultants were not easy and others were. One got to know pretty quickly which were which. The specialisms were broader than they are now; they tended to be more generalist. Mr. Blackly, who was the ENT surgeon, and who needed the finest possible hand-work with ear, nose and throat, had the biggest hands you have ever seen, because basically, he was a sheep farmer! In between operations he would suck his thumb. Then there was Peter Durham, the obstetrician/gynaecologist, who was a dapper little chap - a lovely fellow and a true gentleman.

Going back to pre-modern communications days, when I first started, there were a whole lot of routine visits to be made for various reasons – i.e. injections and dressings - and you had to visit someone within two weeks to sign a death certificate. As a consequence, some people whose health was 'dodgy' were seen frequently. Some were dodgier than others. When I first came I had three regulars every night. There were two 'grannies' who called me frequently, and a male patient who sat is a chair all the time while his wife ran the business and I had to go every night to give him an injection. All three of them lived in Bridge Street, Wye. There was one patient up in Hastingleigh who also had a regular night-time injection; another one off the beaten track was twice a week; and also one who lived in Boughton Aluph needed her dressings changed daily. There were not many nurses then. As district nurses were not employed by us, but from a separate organisation altogether, we had very little recourse to them. The injections needed were mainly for pain relief – pethidine. One of the grannies was not for pain relief, it was because of her son, who, if his mother said, 'I do not feel well,' went straight out and called the doctor. This was nearly every night because she was demanding and he was vulnerable. Routinely, visits to her were at weekends as well as weekdays, usually evenings at 8.00 or 9.00 pm rather than nights. These were left-overs in a way, Mac had got into this habit and one just carried on. It was very convenient that a lot of old people lived in Bridge Street.

I had already been made a partner in the practice when the Balfours left in 1964 and we had an agreement when I joined. Several things were in this agreement. One was that I should purchase their house and the surgery and the price was £4,500 for the house, and £1,500 for the surgery. That was £6,000. Also if either of us were to leave, we would not be able to practice within 10 miles of the Parish Church. Well £6,000 was a lot of money for a house in those days (it was 1960 when I signed my agreement becoming a partner). My solicitor said, 'Well look, it was a bit off to be pinned down to this.' There was no house inflation then – so he altered it in the agreement, to 'valuation at the time' – i.e. the first offer of the house at the valuation at that time, which of course was not a good thing for me in the end, because in the meantime the house had risen to £15,000 and the surgery on the other side was probably £3,000, but fortunately for them I had not signed their agreement, because their London Solicitor was trying to pin us down, you see. That was the one thing that we escaped. That was quite interesting. So when the time came, we could not afford to buy the house. A lot had to be done to it, and so we broke with tradition of centuries as the doctor's house had belonged to the Murray-Jones, and the previous doctors. We could not possibly afford it at valuation, which was to the Balfours' advantage, of course, so it went on the open market and Michael Waterfield bought it and opened the Wife of Bath, which was a great advantage to the village which has benefited ever since.

The former Doctor's House as the Wife of Bath Restaurant

We did buy the flat at 116 Bridge Street from them, then later bought the whole house when Frank Taylor, who lived in the flat downstairs, moved into Orchard Drive. We must have done this at about the same time the Balfours left in 1964. Trish and I then had to convert it into a house again. The whole house was covered in 'brown grain and varnish'. Anyway, we then had a five bedroom house – tiny bedrooms. I think originally they were put up as student accommodation in the Edwardian times. I believe a lot of the students lived out and the original owners of the pair of villas, Fern Villas 1903, had this in mind. We had one of the bedrooms converted into a playroom.

We had a year when the Balfours were still in the district in Boughton Aluph after they had left, and it was very difficult because they were still there but we were running the practice. I had taken on an assistant, John Perry, by that time. Dr Mac had made a ghastly error; he retired a year earlier than he financially should have done. He had made a mistake with his dates. So he had to come and ask me if I minded if he worked in Ashford, which was within 10 miles of the practice, which of course, I did not. So he went back into hospital and did house jobs for a year in order to get his full pension. They decided that they'd had enough, I think.

In the 1960s modern medicine was really just breaking then. At the old surgery, between the consulting room and the waiting room there was a kind of corridor where we kept all the big bottles of medicine of most extraordinary mixtures. We only saw one representative and he provided barbiturates. The medicines we used were all classics. We only had about four antibiotics. There was digitalis folia for hearts, phenobarbitone for blood pressure, and then there were the stock bottles of all the mixtures, Mist Pot Cit (potassium citrate) this, and Mist Sqills that; Mist Morph et Ipecac (Kaolin Morph) was the most popular because I have a suspicion that it was slightly addictive; we only had about three ointments. But people did get better – despite this.

The Balfours left before the really big changes to GP practices took place in 1965. It was still a continuation of the pre-health scheme in general practice; the attitude to general practice was that it was very much hands-on. You were a generalist, you did a bit of surgery, you did everything. It was only when things were beyond you that you went to hospital. People did not expect to go to hospital – their attitude was that you died in hospital. When I started, access to new patients was very restricted. There were restrictions to where one could practise in the area, but funnily enough there did not seem to be restrictions on the town doctors - we still had some people in Wye who were under the town doctors in Ashford.

At that time, Scotton Street had a number of retired widows who had doctors from Ashford – until they went ill. Then the doctors did not want to come out any more, so then they changed. Amongst them were several widows of College staff and Miss Goodwin. Miss Goodwin was very clever. She was very interesting. She had the Diogenes Syndrome like the chap who lived in a barrel. She stored everything, would not give anything away and lived this extraordinary life. When you went into her house she had never thrown a newspaper away for 60 years. She used to sit on a step on a newspaper outside her house and all the students used to stop and talk to her. When she was eventually ill enough to be referred into a hospital and ended up in a nursing home, I went to see her. She was reading Russian novels. I looked after her there.

Miss Hudson ran the farm at the top of the hill towards Hastingleigh. She was a hard task master and I looked after the people that Miss Hudson sacked - the Irish families. They were some of the best patients that I had ever had. They had been treated so appallingly and I did not know what was going on. They appeared and I dealt with them but they had been treated terribly. The fact that they had actually turned up and been looked after was new to them because they had had such a terrible time with her. There were Teehans, Poots, and a chap who was a farrier and lived behind the Coulters, where the forge was.

On one occasion I had a lady who lived in a caravan beside a stream in Brook. She was very independent and had developed a problem gynaecologically. I told her what I thought she had and needed treatment in hospital, but she would not go. She did not like hospitals or their doctors etc. She said she was all right there. So I asked if she would mind if somebody came to see her at her caravan and eventually she said yes. So I rang up Peter Durham, who was the obstetrician of choice locally. He was very supportive to GPs and in those days we did have a system whereby you could have home visits by consultants if you asked them. When they came out on a domiciliary visit, it saved somebody going to hospital if they were perhaps too ill to go. Peter was always fantastic at coming out for something important, and agreed to come. To make it easy, I met him in Wye as it was a difficult place to find and two people meeting at the same spot was often complicated. So I took him out to Brook and it was raining and we walked across the field and over a plank to get to the other side of a stream where her caravan was. He had rather smart shoes on and I wished I had said he could borrow my wellingtons. We went into the caravan and saw the lady, examined her and he absolutely charmed her. Then we went to the other end of the caravan where the lady, very traditionally, (all our old patients knew the right thing to do), had placed a clean towel and a ewer of water to wash our hands. I picked up the ewer jug, poured the water into the ewer and there, in the water, water shrimps were dashing about! The water was straight from the stream. Peter did not turn a hair. But he had charmed her and she went into hospital, had surgery and did quite well. It was the stream that runs from the Devil's Kneading Trough then out of the chalk at Fishponds, then under road and carries on to Brook.

Patient numbers at the practice when we started were about 1500, and when we left there they were about 8,000, mostly from around Wye. Firstly there had been a lot of building that went on. Every village had a Council House estate built in it. Wye had Churchfield Way and then Little Chequers. With it, according to the plans, there had to be a private one built as well, so you got Orchard Drive, Chequers Park, and Jarmans Field as a sort of balance. The same happened in Hastingleigh – Becketts Close, and there is another little bit up there opposite. Mersham was the same and Boughton Aluph. Every village had to have a balance between council housing and private. This was when every house was for three people. Then, when there was a change in GPs' remuneration in 1965, the Ashford doctors no longer needed to come out into the country; they did not like to and they had enough patients in Ashford with all the new build there. We then found ourselves invited further and further afield, partly due to patients who had started off at home and then moved, but did not necessarily move very far, and they would take us with them. For that reason we did have quite a number of patients in Ashford, not because we wanted them there, but because they asked us to go with them. In order to come back into the country, they had to take the first Council House offered to them, which was very often in an urban block, and they would do their stint there and then come back, which was quite interesting.

CHAPTER 11: THE COLLEGE AND THE PRACTICE

Wye College had been opened as the South Eastern Agricultural College in 1894 and then became Wye College[xvii], an Agricultural College affiliated to London University, awarding degrees from 1904. It was taken over by the MOD during then war, and then set up again post-war when Dunstan Skilbeck became Principal. Swanley Horticultural College for women joined the College at Wye around 1949-50, making it both agricultural and horticultural, and Miss Smythe became Vice Principal. At this time Withersdane was created to house the women.

The relationship with the College had been that Mac was the College doctor and he liaised with the Principal, Dunstan Skilbeck. Mac used to go there every day to see him at about 11.30 am for coffee. This was to discuss, quite wrongly in my opinion, the illnesses of the students. Everything was always communicated to Dunstan Skilbeck – who micro-managed the whole place and was informed about everything. The decree was that nobody should be ill for more than three days in the College or they had to go home. Well, a lot of the students, such as foreign students, had not got homes to go to, so around the village we had designated families that would take them in unbeknown to College. One person in particular who was up in Hastingleigh and used to house-sit for the Balfours when they went on holiday, was Granny Forge. She looked after these ill students and as she lived down in the woods, - well out of the way. This was as good as going home. Funnily enough one of the girls whose name escapes me, I think that she was Dutch in origin, had broken her leg and was up there for several weeks because she had no nearby family. At the very last College Ball that we went to years later, she came and said hello to us.

Dunstan Skilbeck, Principal of Wye College

Dunstan Skilbeck was a law unto himself. He modelled Wye College on an Oxbridge-type college. It was fantastic what he did by pursuing this viewpoint, Some of the things he introduced were the wearing of gowns and Senior Common Room dinners. There was always a fixed reason for these dinners where he invited people for a purpose. I think that

Louis Wain avoided them. I think that he was so important to the College that he could get away with anything. The other Professors seemed to defer to the Principal. This is what it seemed to me from the outside. I believe him to have been more of a brilliant and effective leader and administrator than an academic. I think that in the RAF he had been in an administrator position.

I remember going to a dinner with John Ward[xviii] (the artist), and a chap whom I think was the Director of East Malling Research Station. It was all pre-organised; over coffee, after having had the dinner, you then had to earn it, when there was the discussion, led by the Principal. You can guess the question that I had. It was about death, whether it was right to put people down or not. When it came to the easy mode of death, which one describes as euthanasia, the gentleman from East Malling had got a Mother in Law, who was living at home with him, whom he could not wait to get rid of, and after a few jars he was very vociferous about this. John Ward was questioned on how terrible the architecture in Ashford was and he totally disagreed with the Principal's view, and said, 'Obviously you do not go around with your eyes open – just look up above the façades of the shops and you will see the most glorious architecture.' Another topic of conversation was abortion, whether one should only have two children and use contraception. John Ward had got six children, I had got four children, Dunstan himself had got three – so we were not exactly an unproductive group. The dinners were all male do's, or seemed to be. There were very few ladies on the staff then - Jeanne Ingram, Miss Schimmer, and 'Doccy' Smith.

The College was very important to the practice because it filled in the gap between the old and the young. This age group was largely missing in the village. The College had a group of a few hundred students between 18 and 30 years of age, who as far as illness was concerned, did not cause a great deal of concern, but a few had illnesses that were interesting. A lot had travelled abroad so tropical diseases had to be at the fore of one's mind quite often. Not only did a lot of students come from overseas, but also a lot of the staff went abroad and so needed special injections and all sorts of advice and so on and also when they came back if they ran fevers one had to be very alert as to what it might be. We had the odd AIDS case. One chap with AIDS should never have come because he was too ill. I think that he was actually a relation of a Minister from the country from which he came (AIDS arose in the late 1980s and early 1990s).

One day, Mac Balfour was visiting the College and had, unfortunately, parked his little Morris Minor outside. A group of students had then taken it to pieces, taken these through the College entrance, and re-assembled the car again in the College quad. When Mac came to get in his car, it was not there. There was a student at College called Joe Kotsequanl, he was from Lesotho and was a lively character; Joe had been part of this. Joe and his wife made return visits to the College to visit the Balfours and ourselves. They were a lovely couple, he and his wife, Sadie. They came to us for supper once. We remember it as the one and only time that we had a Rolls Royce or Daimler chauffeur-driven car with a flag on the front, parked outside the house. He became Minister of Agriculture for Lesotho. He came back specially to make a visit to College. I think his wife gave a talk to the Women's Lunch Club that Trish started up for young wives, and later his daughter came as a student.

One time, whilst I was working, Trish and I both developed jaundice while the Balfours were on holiday. During the week I had been going off tune and knew jolly well that I had got it. I was off my food and had other symptoms. I remember having sausage and mash and feeling pretty sick after it, whereas normally I would eat well. There was bang, bang on the door in the early hours of the morning and there was a Nigerian chap from College saying 'Doctor, can you come and see my friend Emmanuel? He is not at all well - he has a big fever.' So off I went to see him and there was Emmanuel in bed with malaria, shivering and shaking brrrrrrrrrrrrrr and there am I with a high fever sat on the bed with him and I said, 'I do not know which of us is the more ill!' As the College was often having overseas contact, malaria was not unusual especially with students from overseas who were kind of immune at home, but when they changed climate, it seemed to bring it on. We did stock the relevant medicines in the surgery. My father reacted like this when he came back from Africa. He nearly always had a go of malaria when he came home. So, after this, Emmanuel was my friend forever. We talked frequently. He was always about and I was able to say to him that I was Nigerian and he used to look at me, and I said 'by conception, not by birth'.

I remember an anecdote about Dunstan Skilbeck. Every morning he used to go around the College Farm on his horse checking up to see that the gates were all right and everything was in good order and there was no rubbish. He was very meticulous in having law and order about the place. One morning he was obviously doing this when his horse got its foot trapped in a rabbit hole and threw him. There he was, quite a long way from anywhere. I seem to remember it was along a bank in a field beyond the beagle kennels, somewhere up that way. I do not know quite how anybody found him. Probably his horse went back and they went to look for him and found out where it had come from. It was not quite clear how hurt he was, but he was not happy with his back and his legs and so on. So he obviously had to be got from where he was to the ambulance which had been called and was waiting at his house at Coldharbour.

The Wye College beagles

The ambulance only had two men. The fellow who found him made three - I forget who it was now - and myself, so there were four of us with the stretcher. We had to carry him all the way, and he was not a small man. We eventually got him to his house, where the ambulance was. Then we had a real discussion because the ambulance men said that they were taking him to hospital in Ashford and he refused to go to there. Ashford had a poor reputation at that time, and Canterbury had a better one. There was then a great harangue between him and the ambulance men. I had to intervene and say, 'I think, for everybody's peace of mind, could you take him to Canterbury?' So he went to Canterbury. He would get his own way whatever happened – but not always.

Another time I had a go with him about a student who wanted to get married, not to another student; this was during the course of his last year. The Prin. objected strongly to this. He said 'no, you cannot get time off to get married' and this student came to see me and he obviously was in quite a state. The girl he wanted to marry was actually living in the village with an old lady who lived in Cherry Garden Lane, and always had a lot of students lodging with her. It was where the Nix's lived later. Anyhow, the girl was there - she was a secretary somewhere. As he had come to see me in a state, I went to see the Prin. and said, 'Is this fellow a good student?' and he said, 'he is a good student'. I said, 'well, you know, he is going to give up'. He said, 'it is not a good time for students to get married' and I said, 'well look, I was married as a student so I feel quite strongly about this, and I had my first child whilst I was still a student'. Eventually, he agreed. So the Prin. was get-roundable! I think that Coldharbour (the Principal's house) was renowned to be the noisiest house in Wye. They were pretty noisy. They did not talk, they shouted. They were larger than life.

The railway service was very important then. You might find a load of chicks waiting to be collected and there would be old Mr Coulter the carrier, come down to collect them with his horse and with Marjorie, his right-hand woman, on board. Marjorie had a hard life. Father and daughter were out in all weathers delivering logs or pigs or whatever they did in an open cart. Marjorie was relatively young when she died. We were very upset with the naming of Jarman's Field because Coulter's horse was always there and as far as the villagers were concerned it was Coulter's Field. I think it was called Jarman's Field because somebody looked at an older map. The Coulters had always kept their horses on that field. He had a grand grey horse. The family had been there since the 1600s.

The butcher had been the family butcher, father and son, for some time in Wye. He and another chap were both interested in the same lady and they met out somewhere and had a fight. The Butcher got a great cut over his eye, and he did not win the fight due to this. I was called out by his wife: 'My husband has fallen down and cut himself, doctor, please will you come round and see him.' I went round there and actually stitched him up as he was lying on the butcher's block. He said, of course, that he had fallen over 'when he was taking his dog out!' The other chap 'was taking his dog out' as well! Trish recalled that their daughter Stella was the cashier in a little kiosk in the shop. Poor Stella, we all felt that she was never, ever allowed to go out anywhere and that she would remain a maiden lady for the rest of her life.

When Mr Maxted retired, Mr Wakelin took over the butcher's shop. There was, at one time, Maxted on one side of Church Street and Bugden's the other - now both gone. We remember Bugden's as a wonderful shop, absolutely full of interest. They cut their own ham and supplied the village with sherry, dry or sweet, from two large barrels. Working there were Edna and Jack. He had proposed to her 20 years earlier before they eventually got married. Peter, who also worked there, wore a single earring.

Mrs Akerman had a sort of up-market sweet shop in Wye High Street. Her son Ron ran Olantigh Nursery. Ron was a member of the Caterpillar Club. He had bailed out over Germany quite early in the war and had been a prisoner of war for the rest of the time. His father, funnily enough, had been head gardener at Chilham Castle, so horticulture was in his blood. When he died his widow remained in the village. It was a wonderful sweet shop, with rows and rows of jars. Our children told me there were five shops in Wye where they could get sweets when they were young.

Clockwise from left:
Porker Dodd
Mr Maxted the Butcher
Mr Coulter driving past Holdstocks Store
Mr Coulter driving past Mrs. Brenchley's Baker Shop
Mrs. Akerman in her shop
Mrs. Akerman's sweet shop on the High Street

Miss Pilkington lived in Blue Shutters, opposite the College. She was an Inspector of Schools and a member of Wye Historical Society. She was not a well lady but always in her holidays and after her retirement used to travel around in South America, Jordan, Kashmir and so on along with a group of travelling friends. She had severe heart trouble, but she had great inner strength and was a very keen traveller. So every time she wanted to go away, we had to check her over to see if she were fit to travel and would then say 'yes'. She was also seen by John Lipscombe, a physician at Canterbury Hospital. Eventually he suggested her travels should stop and I was given the task of telling her. So I went along to see her, wondering how on earth I was going to tell her. And I thought, I know how I am going to handle this, I shall say that in the possible case of your demise it would be very unfair on your friends to have to make burial arrangements. So I went to see her after surgery one evening. When I went in she said, 'would you like a glass of sherry ... and I know why you have come'. She went to the bureau and got out a letter and said, 'I think that you ought to read this,' which said something like: 'Dear Dorothy, In the event of a disaster occurring to you on our next trip, we will be very happy to make sure that your body is brought home. etc. etc.' and signed by all her friends. She said, 'I knew that was what you were calling about and this saves you the bother'. She went off on her various trips again; I think that this one was to Kashmir, staying on a houseboat on a lake. I know that she went on a donkey once to Petra.

One evening, at about half past nine or ten o'clock I was called out. 'Doctor, doctor come at once to the car park outside the village hall'. So I went dashing down to find a lot of people standing around a body. Miss Pilkington had come out into the cold and collapsed and died. It was a particularly lovely evening and she lay there in the car park with her friends gathered around her.

Trish reminded me that, on an earlier occasion she answered the phone to British Airways. They said, 'There has just been an emergency landing at Heathrow Airport and we have had to evacuate the plane. We had on board a patient of your husband's called Miss Dorothy Pilkington. We are rather concerned about her because she told us that she has heart trouble – she came down the chute and left all her medication on the plane. We need to know what tablets she is on.' I was in Brook at the time, so Trish rang me with the phone number. I rang the number, which was the medical department of Heathrow Airport, and fortunately I did remember all the medication that she was on, digitalis, frusamil etc. and I said, 'You had better give her a full prescription because I expect she will want to fly out tomorrow, won't she?' They said, 'How did you know that?' So of course she was off again. She would not give up for anything.

At the College there were two brothers, or possibly cousins, called Greenstreet. One of them, I think, was the College groundsman. He used to look after the cricket and rugby sports grounds. He had been in the First World War, and he used to show everybody a tin that he had in his pocket that had been hit by a bullet. The other brother worked in the hop garden. One had retired and lived in a bungalow near Frank Taylor and the other lived in Scotton Street on the right hand side going up. My first meeting with the latter was in the middle of the night when he was delirious. He had pneumonia and was very poorly and his wife was in a state because she could not control him. He was seeing Germans coming out over the trench. Sure enough I looked out of the window, the chimney pots on the other side of the road looked like people coming at him. It was awful. Fortunately he recovered from this. Later, though, he collapsed one day in the hop garden and died. I seem to remember seeing him there and going to tell his wife. Greenstreet is a local name.

During the war, in the field behind the new surgery in Oxenturn Road was the Air Royal Observer Corps base. Volunteers documented the planes coming over. It was staffed by local villagers throughout the war. The chap who was in charge of it was called Allan Baker. He lived in a house called Glenthorne, opposite the New Flying Horse. He was a very interesting chap. He had been in the Colonial Service in Malaysia and was a very knowledgeable fellow and spoke all the languages. When he came back, he was employed by the BBC World Service to answer letters from the Far East and Malaysia. A girl would come down from London every Tuesday and he would interpret the letters and give the answers. There were people from Malaysia who would write letters saying, 'we have heard of Lord Nelson, can you tell us more about him?' He would respond to this. He was married to a lady who was the only person in the village who took the Daily Worker. She used to cycle round with a big basket on the front of her bike. She was an authoress and she gave us a book which the children still have.

During the war, Allan Baker was in charge of the Royal Observer Corps in Wye, and he was on duty with a chap called Porker Dodd (he was known as Porker because his father was a pork butcher). One morning in 1940 they had a radio contact saying, '100 bandits heading your way due north. Will be over you in 3 minutes.' Porker reputedly said to Allan, 'Just time to sharpen our pencils and have a pee, sir'. It was Allan Baker who told me this. He had one son who was a well-known and highly decorated pilot during the war. When Allan was dying, it was this son who came and looked after him and I think he was one of the best nurses I have ever known. He cared for his father fantastically. Talk about an example.

We looked after the Wye races and I was a doctor at the very last race. The village was involved in the races. It was rather sad when they closed it down. It was very interesting on a race day. We were honorary doctors to the meeting, which was supposed to give us kudos in some way. We had to nip out and make visits in between races. At the beginning the care was really absolutely pathetic – the vet had his gun, and the doctor had his morphine syringe and that was about the lot. There was a first aid van organised by St. John's somewhere and personnel at each fence who were not first aiders, so really the medical side was pretty thin on the ground and quite frightening too with falls. At a small race course like Wye trainers are often trying out unknown horses or giving them a run to see what they are like. It was the only race meeting on a Monday and was over the jumps. It had the misfortune to have very sharp corners and, over time, the corners tended to have a camber outwards and falls were not uncommon, sometimes in-between jumps as well. The jockeys were well-known ones like David Mould and Terry Biddlecombe, who became successful trainers. Mould used to ride the Queen's horses. The repartee between the jockeys beforehand always amused me because they used to curse each other in the paddock, but would then be friendly afterwards. The children learned all their bad language from the jockeys. If a chap was carried off with a broken leg he was laid in a tiny little room called the Ambulance room which had a washbasin with cold water and a truckle bed and that was the sum total. A poor chap could be lying there in agony and in could come Mould, who gave him a right row. 'You .... should have done so and so.' The jockey said, 'Sorry David.' Then Mould said, 'Oh all right, that's over then. Right oh! I will ring your wife and make sure that everything is organised for when you get home.'

Taylor's Garage was involved with the winching of horses. They had an ex-army vehicle, a Dinosaur, to deal with any fatalities. Various people were kept busy. The publicans had to order extra beer on the day because train loads came down from London. They put on Specials, originally. Trish recalled the Victoria (now Tickled Trout) being the most popular pub, due to Bubbles, the landlady. George, the landlord, was always a bit morose, but his wife Bubbles was great. She was very involved with village affairs. There was also a beer tent on the site - I think that Bubbles was involved in the bar there. Christine Grace was always there. She was an avid race fan. Although I talk about 'we' at the race course, there was only one doctor there, the second was always on call. I was the official doctor. There were times when I was there on my own, actually, but I still had to nip out between races.

There were various people in Wye who were delegated to clean the loos or be a starter. There was a couple who never left their house and would always send for the doctor to call. They were quite elderly, but on race days they would

OFFICIAL PROGRAMME PRICE 1/-

WYE
STEEPLECHASES
and Hurdle Races
Under National Hunt Rules
MONDAY, 20th APRIL, 1964

STEWARDS
LORD RODERIC PRATT GUY JANSON, Esq.
Lt.-Colonel A. O'B. FFRENCH BLAKE, T.D., D.L.
Colonel H. M. ALLFREY, M.C., T.D., D.L.
Stewards' Secretary—Brigadier S. H. KENT

OFFICIALS
Handicapper—Mr. P. F. J. DUNCANSON
Starter—Major A. GRAHAM
Judge—Mr. C. G. SEYMOUR
Clerk of the Scales—Mr. KEITH S. FORD
Auctioneer—Mr. M. GRIFFITHS
Medical Officer—Dr. G. S. FLACK
Veterinary Surgeons
Mr. P. M. F. SAMBROOK, B.Sc., M.R.C.V.S.
and Mr. J. H. AYLIFFE, M.R.C.V.S.
Clerk of the Course and Stakeholder
Mr. D. J. L. WYATT
Harville, Wye, Kent

PRICES OF ADMISSION
Course 3/-
Reserved Enclosure, including Paddock 17/6 extra.
Public Enclosure 5/- extra. Each Vehicle, any size 5/-.

The Management reserves the right to refuse admission to, or expel any person from, the Racecourse, without assigning a reason for so doing.

Printed by Geerings, High Street, Ashford, Kent.

Clockwise from above:
Wye Steeplechases Race Card giving me as Medical Officer
Wye Races, course and crowd
Wye Races, paddock and crowd

make the race meeting because one did the male loo and the other did the female loo. They could get themselves together to go there because there was an incentive. One day, this couple said to me, 'We think that this will be more use to you, doctor' and gave me a shooting stick, which was rather exclusive and expensive. I thought this was very generous of them and then thought, 'I wonder how he got that?' Then I could see exactly how he had - someone had gone into his loo for a pee and left it behind. I use this stick now, actually. It has been sitting around for years and now that I am getting a little bit slower, I take it with me when I take the dog for a walk and sit and watch the dog run around for a bit.

There were many original Wye villagers and their families who had been doing designated tasks for years because the Wye races had been going on since 1849. The original Wye races were up on the Wye Downs behind the Crown. It was actually a straight course, straight up that valley. There were a lot of jobs to do at a race meeting: the guy that had the numbers to give to the jockeys; and the one who put the numbers of the jockeys up on the big board; and the same men always appeared to do it. Each fence had two chaps to repair it after the horses had gone through. There must have been at least 30 people involved on race day.

Herb Sutton as a Chelsea Pensioner

When we lived in Bridge Street opposite The George, it was also a popular pub. There were some old boys who went there: Jock Jones, Porker Dodd, Herb Sutton and Fred Catt. Herb Sutton lived in a house he owned in Oxenturn Road. He later moved to Audrey Disbury's B&B in Ashford and then became Wye's first Chelsea Pensioner and went to live in the Royal Hospital Chelsea. There were a whole lot of Catts. It was very much a local name. Fred was a first class poacher. They all met at the George to play cribbage. Porker and Fred had been at school together and met at the pub every night at 7 pm. They had two pints and left at closing time. The Hoggs were the publicans then. Sometimes I would be mowing the front lawn outside our house or Trish would be putting up wallpaper in a room at the front and they would come across with a foaming pint of beer. There was a most lovely room at the George upstairs, shaped like an upside-down boat. It went from one end of the house to the other and was ideal for entertaining. If the Hoggs had any family gathering, they would invite us. They had four most beautiful daughters. One married the Head of one of the first comprehensive schools, in Bristol. After Mr Hogg died his wife carried on as the publican.

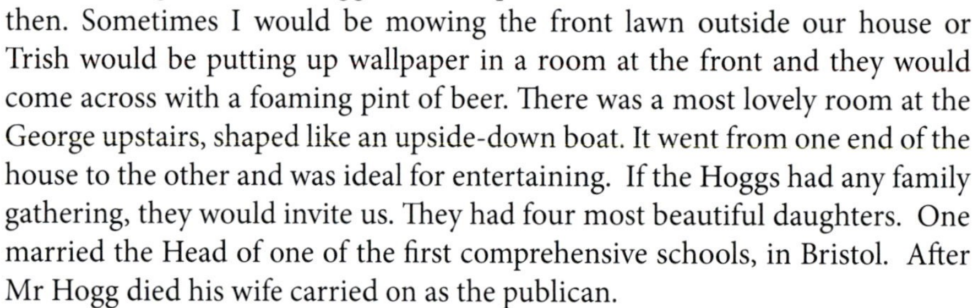

One out-of-the way place which always seemed to throw up trouble was Marriage Farm, above Wye. David Kneen, who lived at Marriage Farm at one time, was a naughty boy, a real rascal. He was handy with a 12-bore and before he was married would stop the local hunt going over his land, telling the Master, 'if they come here I'll shoot the fox in front of you.' I went to the farm one day to see his wife, who was pregnant. This time it was a placenta previa and she had a massive bleed. I carried her out in the pouring rain, stuck her in the back of my car, bleeding profusely, and took her to Willesborough Hospital.

Another time I was called to Marriage Farm to find David sitting in the barn at the bottom of a ladder, surrounded by about 20 sacks. He supposedly had a bad back. And of course, I helped him carry them up. He ran a wreck

Fred and Ruth Richardson, Hassell Street

of a farm, but grubbed out a lot of brambles and increased his farm acreage.

He bought all the remaindered ewes at the market, all very old and lame. He took out their few remaining teeth, which helped them eat better on their gums. Then he put them to the rams. He lost a lot of the old sheep. One day I saw a lorry full of old ewes being taken off for slaughter. But he got plenty of lambs and built up a flock from them. The first time Trish and I went there I remember David had shot a deer and we ate venison. My children used to love going up to Marriage Farm and playing with the Kneen children.

Marriage Farm and Downs Farm were owned by a man called Formaggini. He was Italian, an ex major domo at the Hotel de Paris. He bought Marriage and Downs Farms in the 1920s. He rented the farms out to David Kneen and the Wheelers respectively. He used to bring me a bunch of asparagus in the spring. As an old man he decided to go back to Italy to die and sold the farms to them, as sitting tenants, cheaply.

After Marriage Farm was owned by Michael Waterfield, who started the Wife of Bath restaurant. He wrote *'Leaves from a Tuscan Kitchen'* [xix] there (source of the watercress soup recipe I use) and created a vineyard, which was eventually wiped out by rabbits. After the Waterfields came Chris Nesfield, who had been a successful Point-to-Point trainer, with stables in Charing, and his wife Waveney. They retired to Marriage Farm with their daughter Lindy, husband David, and a brood of children including quads. I remember Trish and I went to their Golden Wedding. They had a new pond and everyone was asked to bring a goldfish. All the local pet shops sold out!

Hassel Street adjoins some of the wildest terrain in the area where unusual wildlife and plants abound. Fred and Ruth Richardson were brother and sister and lived together in a house that had been owned by Miss Hudson. On my first visit to the cottage, which was opposite the flint cottage at the end of Hassel Street and very tumbledown, I was called to Mr Richardson for a hernia problem. I examined him and washed in a bowl in the kitchen sink then emptied the bowl, which went straight into my shoes! There was no pipework and water just flowed outside from the floor. There was an outside loo too. The house was later condemned. They kept chickens and a cow. When the cow died they managed to get a council house in Aldington. They asked if I would like a corner cupboard I'd admired, which is now in the snug, and they gave William a ferret box as he helped with the move.

Ruth always conscientiously protected the rare wild orchids that grew in the surrounding woods. She used to wear a1930s dress of diaphanous material, and moved silently between the trees, obviously knowing every footstep.

About half-way down were Chris and Mike Gorell-Barnes at Hazel Tree Farm. They had a family of lively girls and more than their fair share of tragedy over the years. There was one night when Chris called me out because of a baby's irregular breathing. It turned out to be nothing serious, but I said it was wise to have been cautious. In fact on the drive up, I told her that I had enjoyed seeing all the night wildlife scuttling in and out of the hedges.

An old couple lived in Brook in a four-square house on the right-hand side, surrounded by a few very old sheep. They were on their own, but the daughter lived in a bungalow next door, eventually. They called me out over Christmas one year, it was a 'flu year'. I went in to find them both in bed in a huge old feather bed. He was a little man, she was ampler. Both of them had secondary infections. I examined them and realised they were both very poorly and needed to stay put. I said to the wife, 'Better look after him. He's worse than you. He's blue.' 'I'm not surprised, she said, "he's just been out and fed the sheep." So what could I do? I came back that night and fed the sheep. The husband was very deaf, with solid wax, and I said, "When you're better, come down to the surgery and I'll wash out your ears." He answered "Yes!" (his answer to everything). So when he was better he cycled down to the surgery and the secretions of 80 years came out. "Oh, I can hear!" he said. Eventually ten years later they both died on the same day. I was called out when he died in the morning and again when she died in the afternoon.

Whenever Trish's parents came over I seemed to get called out. A landowner who had retired to farm in Waltham, opposite The Poor House, called me out one of these times. He farmed on his own and had lots of bullocks. He lived in London during the week and came home at weekends. When I arrived he was in his chair in agony with lots of small dogs whizzing around, jumping on the furniture and on him. He had a strangulated hernia. 'Sorry', I said, 'you've got to go to hospital.' 'But I can't go! I haven't fed the bullocks and there are all these dogs'. The son lived miles away and I left him a message. Even so, he wouldn't agree to go to hospital until I agreed to feed the bullocks!

A patient had an arterial leg ulcer for years. It was very painful, he was one of the patients I inherited of Mac's regulars. He was on five evening calls for pethidine administration to help him to continue to sleep. The consultant surgeon in Canterbury wished to operate on his leg, but his wife was not keen for him to have an operation. Encouraged by me, he decided to have it done against his wife's better judgement. Unfortunately, he died on the operating table.

His wife held it against me and gave me hell for 15 years. Her brother, who lived opposite her, was dying of cancer. As I went in the back door of his house, she would go out of the front door. So one day I decided to wait at the front door and caught her and said, 'for Charlie's sake we have got to look after him'. She burst into tears and that was the end of it. She got cancer herself some years later, and I saw her out too.

There were a couple of 'old boys' who told me that they had been at Bodsham School, which was, and still is, I believe, a centre of excellence for primary schools. In their day the headmaster and his wife ran the school. It was a very tiny school, but they obviously got a fantastic education. Nearly all of them went to Grammar School from that village school. These two 'old boys' who lived in the village both told me independently that the school emblem was an oak tree (which is on the uniforms today), and that they were there when they planted the tree – it was for the relief of Mafeking in 1900. They then lived side by side as you go up to Hastingleigh, in the two cottages as you get to the crossroads. (Sue Boxall from the surgery lives there now.) They both went off to the First World War together - one was a machine gunner and the other was a stretcher bearer. They survived it and they were there in those two cottages side by side for years, until they both died.

There was a Greek cartoonist by the name of Papas who used to do a regular political cartoon for the Guardian. He lived in Waltham. He had a very large, old Mercedes car and most days he would be whizzing down the hill from Hastingleigh at 4.15 pm to put his cartoon on the 4.30 pm train to London. In those days you just gave it to the guard at Wye Station and it was taken up to London – there was no problem and the train almost waited for him. He lived well, he smoked and was probably well-oiled when he came dashing down and everyone else took care. He did not cause any deaths, but it was a near thing. Bridge Street was not one-way then.

An interesting thing that I never quite understood was that in Boughton Aluph I looked after three families called Fagg, Ladd and Werger. There were three Faggs, all men, two male Ladds and a sister, and three male Wergers and a sister. I think that one of the Wergers ran the hardware store in Ashford. None of the men married, so there were six bachelors. They were all within 200 yards of each other. One lived in a house on the right as you come up from Wye, another in the old forge as you turn left by the green and the third in a wooden cottage further down to the left. Fagg is very much a Kent name. There was a great Kent wicket keeper called Fagg. There was also a nurse Fagg, the midwife.

CHAPTER 13: THE SURGERY MOVE TO LITTLE CHEQUERS 1964

When I realised that I couldn't afford to buy the Balfours' house plus the surgery across the road and I also knew that new surgery premises were needed. So in 1964 I bought the land at the bottom of the Russels' garden in Little Chequers and we built the surgery there in 1965, after the Balfours had left. It was the first newly designed surgery around. John Perry and Elaine had joined the practice by then and lived in Scotton Street. John Perry had joined as a fixed salary partner (an assistant doctor, not a trainee), a year before the Balfours retired. He had been a GP and had recently come back from Africa. In fact, the first year he earned more than me because he was on a fixed salary and I was on a 1/3 share after expenses were paid. I had no expenses but soon discovered the practice had many!

John Perry and I had a good partnership. We built the new surgery a bungalow. When the building was half finished, the Council decided that we had encroached on their land and said they wanted a third of the value of the land on which we were building the surgery because we were going across their land in order the build the surgery. It was not that we had taken any of it, just that we were going across it. There was a strip of land. Just a yard that belonged to them. The law is that people who own land and buildings have to pay for the access to them, if access is owned by others. Hence at the end of Little Chequers there is a piece of grass that the Council owns, so if anyone wanted to build and needed to cross it, they needed to pay for it. Fortunately we found that they had made a mistake.

I had an extremely good architect; his name was Mr Jackson. He did all the surgery and Churchfield Way. He built the College Science blocks and he also built the Chemist's shop. When all this kerfuffle was going on, he said, 'What do the Council want? Do they want Dr Flack to issue all his patients with pogo sticks so that they can get across to see him?' Actually, it was a very worrying time. What happened was, if you look at Little Chequers, the path runs along the wall of what is now the Chemist's shop, and then you find the road deviates to the left, away from the wall. In the original plans, it should have carried on along the wall but someone had the bright idea that it was better to do that. Of course, this left a gap of land between the wall and the road and our access had gone across it. It was proven, though, that they had failed in their duty in the first place, they should have originally made up the road to the wall and they had not done this. It cost us a £1 actually. It was all so petty, but very worrying at the time. The surgery had been half built by then.

During the course of that building it was the time when we GPs handed in our notice to the NHS[xx]. We wrote to Maidstone in July 1965. GPs up until then never talked to each other because they had all been rivals, fighting for patient numbers. A good illustration was when I was first here, my interest was entomology, butterflies in particular. One day I was driving along Pickersdane to Brook, when I saw a man on the bank with a net, catching butterflies. So I stopped and asked, 'What are you looking for?' and he said, 'small blues'. I chatted with him and he asked who I was. 'Dr Balfour's new assistant,' I said, and he replied, 'I am Dr Scott'. So we said, 'nice to meet you' and so on. Next morning at the 11.00 a.m. meeting I opened the conversation with: 'oh I met one of our colleagues yesterday, Dr Scott.' The reply was, 'We do not speak to him'. I realised then that I had opened a can of worms – there was no communication between the senior doctors at all. This was before the Ashford Medical Society had been formed. Dr Scott had evidently 'poached' some of the practice patients. I understood that Dr Murray-Jones had been called up during the war, into the navy. While he was away the practice evidently fell apart. Various private doctors poached the patients and when he came back there were just a few left who had not bothered to change lists, who Mac and Ana inherited. So it was no wonder the Balfours were not very keen to socialise, because the Ashford doctors had been involved in this. Dr Scott actually came from Westwell.

But the resignation issue in 1965 got us all together. We had a meeting in Ashford of all the young doctors and assistants. We all got on well together and we started the Ashford Medical Society and started meeting regularly. In fact the Ashford Medical Society was solely a social medical support group across the Ashford area and we all joined it. As time went on, it became more of a medical social and sports group. It only ceased to function a few years ago.

We did not just threaten to resign in 1965, we all wrote to say we WILL resign on a specific date unless certain conditions are met. As a result the Government produced the Doctors' Charter in 1966[xxi]. It included clauses that:

- Increased recruitment to General Practice
- Reduced maximum patient lists to 2,000 per GP
- Improved medical education, orientated to General Practice
- Introduced direct reimbursement of staff and premises expenditure
- Made payments to reflect workload, skills, and responsibility
- Set reasonable working hours
- Gave proper remuneration for out-of-hours work (between 9 pm and 7 am)

This led to the establishment of the famous 'Red Book', which increased in complexity over time.

It was very good for us actually, because we then got a lot of financial incentives for the surgery which I was already building. Another small but useful outcome was with syringes. In the old days we used to have glass and metal syringes and we used to boil them up in a saucepan on a gas ring, in the same way that we used to test the urines for sugar. This would be considered primitive now. We used to take haemoglobins ourselves and look at them in the light and compare them. We did not have a steriliser then. The syringes cost a lot but only lasted about three boilings before they cracked. Then a new thing came out – plastic syringes, throw away ones, with needles that you put on. You could buy 20 plastic ones for the price of a glass one. So as soon as we moved to the new surgery I started buying these – and then suddenly the State paid for them. We also got paid for night calls, and I think the mileage allowance went up – in the country we had mileage units. This was absolutely right and was implemented by the Labour Government who could see the dilemma that faced us.

Various things did happen to doctors' practices. Shortly after coming to Wye, Kent and Canterbury Hospital was becoming a centre of excellence, or trying to be. The new University of Kent was set up in the mid-1960s and Canterbury were canvassing to get a medical school in the university. So they set up a post-graduate medical centre at Canterbury Hospital. This was a group of youngish doctors who met weekly – it must have been in my trainee year. So every Tuesday afternoon, I went to Canterbury for lectures and things. This was the first post-graduate further training for GPs in the country, I think. It was an official, properly organised centre but you did not have to go. It was voluntary. Unfortunately, the new University Medical School never took off. There is still a post-graduate centre in Canterbury. Otherwise, after you qualified there was no access to post-qualification in-service training for GPs.

As time went on, following the changes in the mid-1960s for GPs, we had to do so many hours per annum of post-graduate learning. Unfortunately, anything extra-medical was usually in the evenings, in our time, and not in practice time. I was also the lone GP on various health committees at the hospital, including an organisation called Cogwheel, which met at a different hospital every time.

There were changes taking place at that time in surgery organisational culture. The new surgery, initially, was financially an albatross round my neck. It consisted of a waiting room and a reception, two consulting rooms and a treatment room, one of the first built. There were two toilets, one for patients and one for us. Between the two consulting rooms was a dispensary. The office was the reception to start with, but it was later extended three times

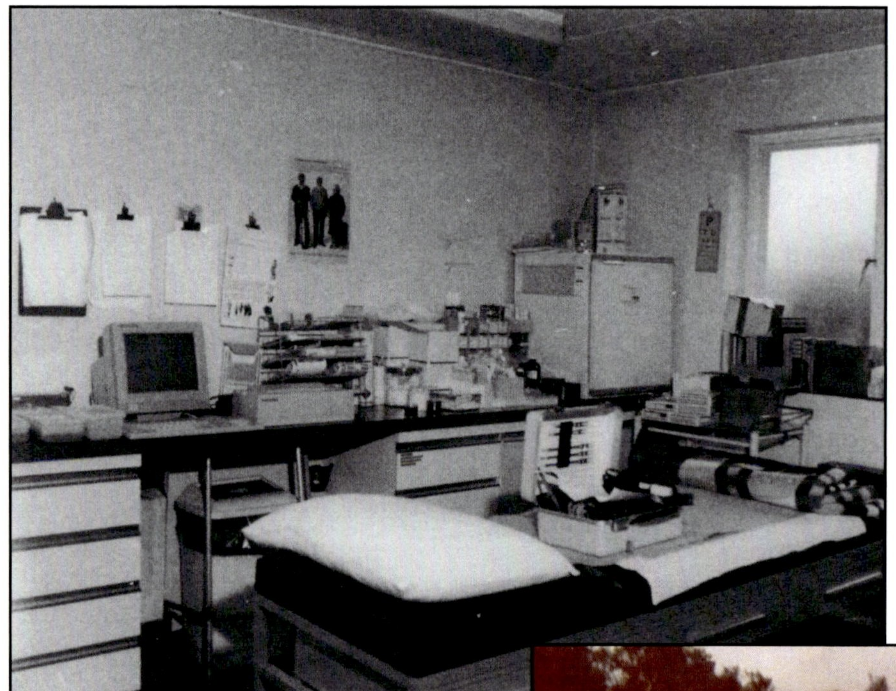

The Treatment Room for GPs and Nurses, Little Chequers Surgery

Below: Little Chequers Surgery up for sale in the 80s

on the site. The treatment room was the biggest room and well used – we did all our own stitching up etc. The nurses, when available, also used it. I think we might have put another consulting room on; we certainly put another office on. The surgery, architecturally, could easily have been converted into a bungalow, if things had not worked out. It is interesting that that was exactly what happened when we eventually sold it. It became a bungalow for a while and then the bungalow was sold back as a dentist's surgery.

One needed a way in which to change the attitude that existed in the old surgery where the consulting room had a two doors system. The patients came in from the waiting room into the consulting room and afterwards they went out of the other outside door into the street. But the 'great and the good', who considered themselves private patients, (though under the NHS they were not) knocked on the outside door to be seen. In the new surgery, we built a decent surgery and started an appointment system. That flummoxed the lot – that fixed it. That was the only way one could think of to foil that system for good. (Trish always pointed out that I was the first doctor in the area to start an appointment system – the others followed on pretty quickly.)

There were a lot of changes, which were not easy. On principle, I did not take private patients. I could not see how it could work in the country, where everybody knew everybody else and one could give no better care than you were giving to all alike. Equally, I think that the 'great and good' realised that it was to their advantage because medicine was not cheap. I assume this is still the case.

Wye was in a special position being on the edge of both the Canterbury and Ashford hospital catchments. So we were able to select the best treatment for patients based on our knowledge of the two hospitals. For instance, Canterbury had an exceptional specialist for obstetrics and gynaecology and there was a very good general surgeon at Ashford.

When I inherited Mac's job as the Doctor to Wye College, I did not go to coffee with the Principal, as this was something of a tradition to be broken, but the students were still queuing up outside what was called the Medical Room. So they continued to have no privacy and confidentiality was lost. I do not think that our relationship with the College changed at all after the move to Little Chequers. I think that we had a good relationship with the College I do not think there were difficulties. But one of the big things was the change from the past of the doctor going into College every day as I felt this was totally wrong. Also I felt that for them, consulting in College was almost escaping because they did not have to queue for long.

Instead of the doctors doing their consultations with students in the Medical Room, and because we had the new surgery, I suggested that students should be treated like any other patients. They were part of the village when they were here; I did not think that they should have any privileges by being seen in a different room, so they had to make appointments and be seen as for other patients; it was important that they integrated with the community – and, reluctantly, this was agreed to. At a later date, Jean Andrews became nurse practitioner at the College and dealt with many student problems with discretion and confidentiality.

I think that there was some incentive for looking after a residential college, some arbitrary sum, but I am not sure. I think we got paid some sort of retainer of £150 per year to be around for the College, but the students had to register with us or if they did not they became temporary residents, so we had the per capita payment. They were supposed to register as they were spending more time at College than they were at home, so they should have been registered patients. This was always a very difficult thing because the moment you register with a doctor, this then has to be sent on to – with us it was Maidstone – who then got in touch with their home doctor through the NHS hierarchy administration, so it had to go round the houses and by the time we got the notes, six months or a year had gone by. It was a terrible system. There were four chances for the notes to get lost or held up somewhere. Then, or course, when they were back at home for their holidays, either the doctor at that end took them on as a temporary resident again, or they tried to re-register them.

The 1960s were a big time of change and John Perry and I had a good partnership for 7 or 8 years after the Balfours left. However, he still had 'the call of Africa' and he went off to Swaziland. That was a sad split. I was then left on my own for a very short time.

Between us, the Perrys and we had 8 children. They grew up together. Jonathon had been born in 1960 and William was born in 1964. We had a Swedish au pair then named Asa. She ran the house whilst Trish visited the hospital and she became a godmother to William. We were busy with four children, but we had this wonderful Swedish girl as well, then. One of Trish's recollections was that the children had a lot of white mice and put an advert in the Post Office , 'For Sale – white mice, sixpence each', and we had a queue of local kids with their boxes for white mice.

In 1963, our daughter Caroline, aged 8, was knocked down by a car in Churchfield Way. She said she had been racing the bus. Trish was pregnant with William when this happened. The car was driven by Mrs Wilkinson who was going to Canterbury to get some clothes for her newly adopted child. We had helped with the adoption of her two children. She was in a terrible state. Someone picked Caroline up and put her on the grass in the rain. Someone else came out of their house and picked her up, carried her indoors and put her in their front room on a settee – all they could see was the hole in her head, not realising that she had a broken arm and broken femur and possible ruptured kidney. She was in hospital for I do not know how long – 3 months. It is the story of our lives that we are deemed to be fortunate, we consider ourselves lucky. Captain Bird, our next door neighbour in Bridge Street, was a strange man, he had obviously had a terrible First World War. He had a wife who was a moon worshipper – totally demented, but gentle. He looked after her but had to have all his meals at the Kilns cafe – breakfast and lunch every day. He had two cars, a Wolseley and a Rover and every day he made the car available for Trish to go to the local hospital. When Caroline went to East Grinstead for plastic surgery he lent us his Wolseley so that Trish could go and see her – we could not have afforded a second car. She was in and out of hospital for about a year.

CHAPTER 14: THE COMPREHENSIVE PRACTICE

General practice then was 24 hours a day. There was no alternative and everybody was either on duty or off.

At home, our wives were responsible for getting hold of us at night. The whole family was involved in the practice. If Trish was caught up with something, the children took the messages and it was a family helping to provide a family service. They were all involved. One Christmas we decided to give Marianne a toy telephone exchange made of tin, where you plug in the phones. She had heard the remarks I had made before I answered the phone, and I and the au pair overheard this little voice saying loudly 'Blast the phone!' And then a sweet voice saying '812414, Dr Flack's house'.

There were two ageing men with the same name who lived opposite one-another. They were both, at times, poorly. The children called one 'Wasp H' because he once dealt with a wasps' nest we had in the roof – he knew everything and was a general odd job man and 'fixer'. The other chap had the misfortune to have a catheter fitted permanently which frequently became blocked. His wife would send a message 'can you come and see Mr H because his catheter is blocked'. The children used to take these messages, calling them 'Wasp H' and 'Catheter H'.

One day on my rounds some distance away, I got a call, 'Dr, Dr come at once, Mr H is not up to much'. Patients were always one of three things: they were 'not up to much', 'I can't do a lot with him' or 'he has gone awful quiet doctor' and that could mean anything from nothing to death. Well knowing that Catheter H was dodgy, I jumped in my car and drove straight to his house; and there he was sitting by the fire, with his feet up looking very comfortable saying 'how nice of you to come, doctor'. So realising that this was not the call, I said, 'well that all right, nice to see you too, I just wanted to check on you,' then nipped across the road to find Mr Wasp H was deceased. He had gone up for his afternoon snooze. When he had not come down at 4 pm his wife went upstairs and found 'he was 'awful quiet doctor' – so he had died, so that was that. The next time I went to see Catheter H he just grinned all over his face and said 'you thought it was me didn't you'.

Trish remembered a funny story which involved a patient. The phone rang in the middle of the night and it was for a patient who had gone into labour. They lived in Tritton Fields in Kennington. I had left and gone to the old surgery to collect the 'Midder Bag' because I always went with my equipment just in case of complications. Just after I had gone the phone rang again – it was about 2 or 3 am. This time it was a call from another woman who also lived in Tritton Fields. Her husband had gone into a diabetic coma. So Trish ran out with her nightie on, stood in the middle of Bridge Street outside our house, waving me down. I stopped and she said you will have to go to the diabetic first, he is the more urgent. But I did get to the other patient before she had the baby! This was a long time before mobile phones, of course.

In the practice, we always had mental health patients who took up a lot of time, as they needed seeing regularly. The trouble was (and it is no different now), that while they are being treated with the appropriate medication, they are fine. After a while, they think 'ah, I am fine' and they stop taking it. So you try to give them regular appointments to come, and then they miss the appointment and you chase them up but they have 'got away' again. This is still true. When St Augustine's Mental Hospital closed there was a gap in provision; we did not know what to do with the acute patients who often ended up under the care of the police. In fact, the kindest people were the police. It was part of the police that one did not realise - they were extraordinarily empathetic towards mental illness and the police station was the place where a lot of acute patients went when St Augustine's closed, until they were seen by the psychiatric services in the cells.

One always had about four mental health patients who became acute from time to time, usually the same people, and one spent a lot of time with them. I had my first experience of needing to certify a patient which really upset me as I had never certified anybody in my life. Some of these patients I had been seeing regularly and knew them, their family, and their backgrounds and what they had experienced, very well. So I understood where they were coming from when other people thought they were well away talking randomly about 'rubbish'.

On occasions, however, there came a time when patients had to be certified: sometimes their close support systems were exhausted. In those days you had to get a JP and a duly appointed officer who was a layman appointed by the council. . The layman used to organise the hospital admission and the ambulance, plus two men in jackets (white coats), which was not easy. I had to arrange the attendance of the local JP and the duly appointed lay officer with ambulance and two men round the corner. You had to get everybody there at the right time, which was the trouble if one party were missing. The process was that the JP talked to the patient and then made the decision and signed a bit of paper. I was very reluctant to certify a patient, and hoped that they might say 'no', really, but when a patient was ranting in their normal manner, JPs and lay people would hardly get over the 'threshold, take one look, walk out of the door, sign the admission certificate, and that was it – off they went, in those days, to St Augustine's. There were times when our acute mental health patients were up, and times when they were down, and some literally, good times, when we would enjoy socialising together.

I rarely certified anybody. I used to persuade people to admit themselves voluntarily. One patient ill with pneumonia, had once become 'delirious and more than confused'. He went ballistic threw all his clothes off and rushed out into the snow, which rather upset the neighbours. I managed to persuade him to come back in and dealt with him. He recovered in a couple of days, but neighbours complained. My partner, (Mac), was persuaded by various people, including a woman who took exception to him, so Mac told me I had got to certify him. But I never had to as he went in voluntarily, which was always the best option if one could. So honour had been satisfied, but there was really no need for him to have gone at all because by the time he went in he was better. It was the illness that had caused the problem.

We had another patient who self-harmed. One of the most intelligent women I have ever met. She was a mature student and had two children. Trish got a phone call from London, and she had slit her stomach with a knife, right across. She said, 'I am about to get on the train to Wye, what are you going to do about me?' Trish said 'well, I shall contact my husband and come down to meet you'. So we went together, scooped her up and took her to the surgery. The extraordinary thing was that she was actually an in-patient at the Maudesley in London and they were sending her home for the weekend. So on the train she had got a scalpel out. Trish was rather surprised at what treatment I undertook with patients in the surgery. We stitched her up and Trish came to give me a hand. We had to. Eventually she went into St Augustine's hospital after slitting her wrists. She got better, went to Australia and became very successful.

Things did not always work out smoothly. I remember another time…people always tended to throw their clothes off, I do not know why. There was a girl in Crundale who did this and the neighbours opposite had had enough of it. She had been out all night shouting and so forth, keeping everybody awake. Every time I went to see her she was fine. She lived with an aged Mother. There came a time when you did not have to get a JP, you could certify as a doctor with a Mental Health Social Worker. So I arranged to meet him at 12 o'clock on Saturday. Along he came, ambulance around the corner. I went in to see her and as I went in the door, she went out of a window, stark naked, and the last we saw was her running up the hill out of Crundale and over a stile. My last vision was of her bare bottom as she disappeared over the style. So we said, 'let's go home, there is nothing we can do about it'. Funnily enough, that girl too did very well eventually. She was wise enough to go into St Augustine's for the winter, more or less self-referred. She came out, got a little dog and that kept her out of hospital. I also remember going to St Augustine's with one particular lady who knew it well and she just took me by the hand to the ward she was going to go to.

In those days the presumption was always that the first point of reference was the GP. We did what we were capable of and triaged as we saw fit. I remember one night that I went to a chap who had had a fall. He lived in the road where the Nailbourne flows which starts at the bottom of Dean Hill, flows beyond Petham then runs along the foot of the hill. On the right hand side there is a farmhouse, Little Bucket Farm, and the chap there fell down and got a terrible cut. It had obviously gone through an artery and he was bleeding all over the place. I went out to him and it was just normal to carry surgical gear as well as everything else and clipped the artery and then thought well, it needs more than I could do, so took him into the Casualty Department at Kent and Canterbury Hospital and there was no Casualty Officer there – there was nobody on. So as I was a volunteer for cover in an emergency there, they provided me with a white coat and name-tag, and I stitched him up and took him home again. One thought nothing of it and did not know any different.

Lordy Hollands

Funnily enough, when he died, that family moved and had a sale which Trish and I went to. He was a great collector this old boy, and one thing I wanted to buy was his fantastic collection of butterflies. He had cases of them – proper cases. But they were out of our league price-wise – way out. But while we were there we bought three Imari vases. Two smaller ones and one bigger one. I do not think that we bought anything else, but we thought that we had better buy something whilst we were there. I still have them.

Lordy Hollands I have many tales about. He was a bit of a pain. Hollands

Canon David Mattiot, Rector of Wye

had the milk round before and during the war. The dairy was at Withersdane. When you go behind Withersdane, there are quite a few little farms down there, owned then by various Hollands and Longs. There were two Longs in a place called Spiders Castle, which was at Naccolt, and John Long and Bedo Long who had the racecourse.

Anyway, Lordy Hollands lived at the back of Withersdane amongst the Longs and the Hollands and one of the Longs married a Holland. He somehow or other managed to upset everybody. His relations could not stand him, we were amused by him, but the relations really had a thing about him. There was some dispute over land that had caused animosity. I think it was where Little Chequers is now. It was a cherry orchard and had belonged to the Hollands. I have never had proof but I think that he sold it extremely well and kept all the money for himself.

If he stopped you, you were due for a long stay. He just would not stop talking. One time, it was a lovely sunny day, and I was outside our front door when we lived in Bridge Street, and I saw David Marriott coming up on his bike as he often was, and we were having a chat, quite sensibly - he looked after the souls and I looked after the bodies, and he suddenly said 'I am off' and he jumped on his bike and cycled off, and the next think I knew, there was Lordy Hollands, and that was that (and I have never forgiven David for it, rest his soul!) . Around this time, I remember an old ex-missionary in Wye saying to me 'you do not have to love everybody you know, you just have to care for them'.

Lordy also had a shop (which is now gone) on the left hand side as you go into Little Chequers. It is now exposed as the end of the Elizabethan house there. It was a real old-fashioned sweet shop selling liquorice and sherbet. He had a timid wife and treated her badly. I had no time for him because of this. She and Daisy Baggott served in the shop. Daisy was another character. Just before we arrived, the Old Flying Horse pub shut; it was bought by the College. It had been run by two old ladies, at least one old lady ran it and her right hand helper was Daisy Baggott. The pair of them left the Old Flying Horse and moved into a bungalow in Little Chequers where I looked after them both. The old lady died and Daisy Baggott, who was a busy lady, always looking for things to do. She worked in Holdstocks for some of the time, and also helped Lordy Hollands in the sweet shop. The kids always went to the shop when she was there because she always gave them more. Lordy gave them less.

Lordy Holland's sweet shop, Bridge Street

The terrible tale about Lordy is that he fancied himself as being a soldier in the First World War and used to go on about being in the Guards. I gather actually that he was in the Pioneer Corps, attached to the Grenadier Guards, but am not sure. He inveigled himself into some army unit meeting they had monthly or bi-monthly. They used to meet at the pub at Lower Hardes, which is no longer there, the Three Horseshoes, and I got a phone call at 10 o'clock one night. 'Major Bloggs here, I am in the Canterbury Hospital, the accident centre, I thought that I had better report to you that Mr Hollands has died. We were at our meeting and he collapsed and he has been taken to Canterbury Hospital and he is deceased.' I said then, 'well what about his wife?' He said, 'what about his wife?', and I said 'well she will be with him. She will be sitting locked in the little A40 car in the car park'. He said 'oh, oh', I said 'he takes her out and makes her go whenever he goes out of the house and she will be there waiting for him'. This is what he used to do, I knew this. She could not drive, she used to sit there with her handbag – she had early dementia you see. Trish thought she looked like the cartoon of Granny in Giles with her hat and her handbag. She was a very gentle lady who would never hurt a fly. If he went out, he took her with him and expected her to wait. I thought that she must have been the auntie to Betty Long, so I got hold of Betty and she was an absolute dear, a super person, and she obviously sorted Lordy's wife out eventually – got them to bring her to her house and then she looked after her. She might have sat in the car all night.

Lordy was a naughty old boy. He became quite unfit to drive a motor vehicle. He came to me for an examination to get his driving licence renewed – for me sign up to say he was fit to drive and I said, 'it is not worth examining you Lordy because I will fail you'. Everybody knew that he was an absolute menace on the roads. There was a fee involved and I said I was sorry and it would have cost him a tenner for the medical and I said, 'I know I am going to fail you because you have driven into so many cars'. He was very angry and disappeared. I next saw him driving. I challenged him and he said, 'I went privately'. So he had gone into Ashford and got it signed by someone who did not know him.

It was Betty Long who rang me to ask if we wanted to buy the piece of land for the surgery. Also, after the death of Lordy, Mrs Hollands had her reward and lived happily in the best care home money could buy.

Trish had a wonderful occasion with dear Mrs Holland. The surgery manager rang her from the surgery to say, 'Trish, I have got a problem, I have Mrs Hollands here, and she has her wedding ring which is cut so far down into her finger because her hands are so swollen, that she has a terrible infection in her finger, right down to the bone'. Lordy had ignored it. I thought that, even if I had a ring cutter, I do not think that I could cut it off. I did not have a ring cutter, but there was a jeweller, in Hastingleigh at the corner of Hassell Street in a little bungalow. I was busy as it was during surgery, and Trish took her up there and bless him with great difficulty, he managed to cut this ring off, but her finger was terribly infected. The jeweller told Trish, 'I am not going to do that ever again – you had better have the tools' and he gave me the ring cutter. So I had the ring cutter and every now and again, A&E would ring up to say can we borrow your ring cutter. In fact on one occasion, which is quite incredible, I had to go into the surgery late one night and I walked into one of the shelves and cut myself, and I thought I had better stitch myself up. I looked in the mirror and just could not do it. Then the phone rang and it was the casualty department saying, 'we understand that you have got some ring-cutters.' This was in the early hours of the morning and I said 'yes', and then said to them 'well its a deal, because you can stitch me up'. We did eventually have to get a new set because the old ring cutter wore out. It had been well-used. It is a jeweller's tool really. It is very clever, it is just a sharp cog wheel, rather like a secateurs, you put one bit of it underneath the ring and then on the top of it you press down and there is a very sharp wheel with indents, and you just keep on doing it and being gold, it is soft enough and you wear it through and then with a tiny pairs of pliers open the ring out and get it off. So you have two pairs of pliers and the ring cutter – three implements.

At the new practice, we always maintained the same responsibilities, but things kept being added on. It was not just an increase in number of patients, medicine was changing: it was going from an art to a science. I think that it is now all science and very little art. Before, one did not have so many tools to treat patients; the medicines that we had were often placebos, the antibiotics were few, and treatment for blood pressure was really non-existent. Most investigations had to be initiated through the hospital. The patients expected you to look after them, and only went to hospital for something really dire. In a rural practice it was family orientated in two respects: patients' families and the participation of GPs' families. The expectation was that you cared for patients from birth to death. I did not know anything different, and that had been my predecessor's attitude.

There was growth in patient numbers because there had been a lot of building over the years within the East Ashford Rural District Council and all around. In a town there would be 30 doctors sharing the patients, but out here there was just one practice, and so for every household, which is equivalent to three people, they were all ours and we had a monopoly without realising it. One reason why doctors did not come from Ashford was because they did not like the railway crossing. Also we had a policy that if patients moved away from Wye and asked if we would continue with them. We always said yes. We considered ourselves to be an outdoor practice.

Early on, district nurses, who were from the District nursing pool, came and went. At one time we did have a nurse attached to the practice temporarily and then the District changed policy and suddenly they were not. Then we employed a nurse, in fact one of the ones that we employed as a practice nurse years ago was Jean Andrews. Then, as the College was looking for a College nurse, we said, well OK as it was to our advantage for Jean to be the College sister and us to employ somebody else, which we did – but that was later on. As well as being paid per capita for patients, we got extra money through doing things like baby clinics for the District in the big village hall, (with curtains for privacy), before the little hall was built, and we held things there like polio clinics.

To start with, for some time, the Practice GPs were myself and John Perry. Amanda Hettigan (Webster) then joined us part-time. The early intention was that Amanda would become a partner, but she decided to have children and retire gracefully for the time being. As we then took on other partners, she eventually went to Willesborough.

Then, when John Perry left, I was suddenly left on my own. It did so happen that (as is quite common in practices) there had been a little bit of a difference between some partners in the South Ashford practice. The two senior partners fell out and they split up acrimoniously. Rob Johnson had been taken on in the practice, I think as an assistant. One of the partners contacted me because they said that they had heard I was looking for somebody and that is how Rob came to us. He came before Ian Nash who had been in a practice in Rye. Ian joined us later and that made three of us.

Prior to Ian Nash joining us, we had started an accident and emergency service. It was called 'K.A.R.E.S., Kent Accident, Rescue & Emergency Service. A lot of things had happened in the District, there were a lot of changes. They had shut down Ashford Casualty between 5 pm to 9 am, so there was no overnight casualty service in Ashford. It meant that everything, including casualties, and road traffic accidents, had to go to Canterbury because, at that time, Canterbury was the centre of excellence around here medically. In a rural practice one tended to attend all emergencies, both medical and accidents, in one's own patch (ours covered an area of 100 square miles), we were known by the Ambulance Service for being involved, and had an association with them. We attended all kinds of incidents including road accidents all round the place. I remember that there was an aeroplane crash and two were killed in Elmsted. Patients also tended to ring the local doctor first in an emergency because they knew that it would take 20 – 30 minutes, at least, for an ambulance to come. Knowing that we were just down the road this is exactly what would happen, it was part of rural practice. As a consequence, the ambulance people were so used to us being present in our own patch when they arrived and dealing with things they asked us if we would help them out.

Ashford Hospital had closed overnight as they could not get the staff. Anyone from the Marsh to Tenterden and Lenham and anywhere was transported to Kent and Canterbury, which was a very long way for critically injured people. Ashford Ambulance Service, on occasions, rang up Wye Surgery and said, 'we are really worried about a patient we have got on board, could you possibly come and have a look at him because we do not think that he is going to make it to Canterbury'. Ambulance people were not medically trained then. Rob and I always aimed to get them to Canterbury Hospital alive. That is what started it. We were the first ones in Kent to provide an accident emergency scheme. It was not just an emergency accident scheme, it was also an emergency scheme.

When ambulances had to drive from the Marsh to Canterbury, for example, with casualties, we used to wait at Boughton Corner and go with the ambulance. People do not realise how highly trained the ambulance personnel are now when they are paramedics. At that stage they were not paramedics, they were a driver and an attendant. The equipment they carried was zero - a stretcher, a few bandages and things – just first aid. They were first aiders. When we started the 'K.A.R.E.S. we got resuscitation gear, transfusion gear, and all the various equipment for 'immediate care'. The important thing was that the equipment that we had was just as much use in our practice as at accidents etc. Trish shared the knowledge that if someone – even maybe a child - in an ambulance was not going to make it and was in 'status asthmaticus', I would rush into Canterbury with it, because I could give them oxygen and injections which the ambulance crew could not do, then the person had a better chance of surviving, whereas if I had not gone with the ambulance they probably would have died on the way. That was really what got the scheme going – it saved a hell of a lot of lives but this was hard to prove. The equipment we had was used universally – although the popular thought was 'Wye Doctors – roadside accidents', but actually the equipment was for immediate care, which meant anything. It could be when somebody collapses, faints or has a heart attack or a big bleed, we had the wherewithal to deal with it on site which was something a bit unusual. But honestly we had been doing it before anyway, but with inadequate equipment.

If there was a road accident, one just certified someone dead if they were. It was very interesting because the Coroners have their own districts, which are fixed, and they are extremely covetous of their own areas. Bodies could not be taken from one coroner's area to another. A Coroner's area is where someone is certified dead, this dictates where they are going to be seen by which Coroner. What was happening when we first did the road emergency accident scheme was that if we went to a road accident in Ashford and certified someone dead, they went straight to the Ashford morgue and therefore it was the Ashford Coroner. This was probably the area where most of their family was as well. But if, on the other hand, someone was killed on the road and taken to Canterbury, they were then certified dead in Canterbury and it came under the Canterbury Coroner so that all their family and all the police etc. who were involved had to go over there despite living in the Ashford area. Had the accident happened locally to us, none of the witnesses or family would have needed to go to Canterbury. So we were very popular because if we certified death by the roadside at Ashford, it saved people an awful lot of trouble. It sounds silly, but it was quite important and people were quite grateful for the fact that they had not got to go elsewhere for the formalities, and it helped save a hell of a lot for families.

Rob had a very distinguished vehicle, which these days we would probably call a Range Rover with flashing lights. About that time we also got onto the same ambulance net with radio telephones. The radio telephone went to whoever was on call and had a little box which we took from house to house. Our wives were on call with this radio telephone affair. This was 24 four hours a day, 7 days a week, and it worked. K.A.R.E.S continued until paramedics were employed by the Ambulance Service and there was no need for us then.

Trish believed that it started with one of the bosses of Taylors Garage having a heart attack in Bridge Street, and if they had had the right equipment, he might have survived. It might also have helped a boy who drowned in the river; they were all patients. I have a suspicion that my own interest in starting K.A.R.E.S. was probably influenced by Caroline's accident as a child when she got knocked down and it could have helped. Things were not good when something did happen as the ambulance was at least 30 minutes away. It was a personal thing which made me enthusiastic about it. Wye has always been very accident conscious. When it is your friends and patients around Wye who die, and they might have been saved, it affects you. Trish believed it saved many, many, lives. I would not know for certain, probably the morbidity was better; people arrived at the hospital better for our treatment.

K.A.R.E.S. was totally self-funded. It was very well supported by the patients and the village and people were very generous. They had raffles and goodness knows what for us. We also had a very friendly bank manager who gave us an

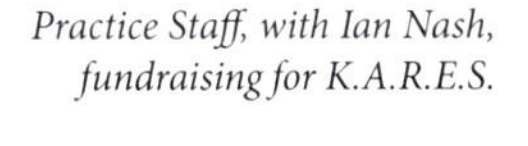

Practice Staff, with Ian Nash, fundraising for K.A.R.E.S.

interest-free loan. What this meant was that if we wanted some equipment we could buy it then and there, and then pay it back as the money came in. What would normally happen is you have to wait until you have got the money to buy the equipment. So we bought the equipment first and paid afterwards. This made a lot of difference. The equipment was always very expensive – defibrillators and so forth - but it was for heart attacks and general use as well. For some reason or other we seemed to have several bank managers on our list who all lived in Wye. They were very helpful. The one who I don't think was our patient was the Lloyds manager who lived in the village. He looked after the finances of the scheme. On two occasions I made a right mess up of trying to be too clever by half. One was a road accident which happened up the top at Challock in the middle of the night (as always). There was the car, with bits and pieces strewn over about 100 yards, which had eventually come to rest in a ditch. In it was a gentleman, who had, by that time, slipped right back into the back. He was all right so we got him out and off he went to hospital. I was worried because I knew that he was two-timing his wife and probably there should have been two of them in the car. We spent a long time looking all over the place for the second party. It was later discovered that they had just been in the pub down the road in Charing. But before I knew what had happened, I was concerned as to whether the woman, whom I knew well, was all right, and the only way to find out was to ring up her home to see if she was there. I rang the phone and she answered it, so I just put the phone straight down. I had been right, they had been together for the evening, but they had separated at the pub, one went one way and the other went another. That was one occasion!

The other one was also for a Challock patient. The police had rung me up to say that there had been a crash near Lower Hardres of all places, involving a Jaguar, and the driver was dead. I was on call and had been on my way to the accident when they said do not bother. They had looked up the car registration and it was so and so. They asked if I knew him. I then went to the house to notify the wife that her husband had been killed in a car crash; knocked on the door and the chap himself opened the door to me. His car had been stolen and the thief had crashed and killed himself. I was very shocked, but also very relieved.

When Dr Nash came in the late 1960s the three of us were very busy, then we got busier still because we became police surgeons as well. I cannot remember the date of that. The police surgeon retired and the police in Ashford, for some reason or other, approached me. Although it was quite a well-paid job, none of the Ashford doctors wanted to do it. That did increase our, mostly nocturnal, activities. A lot of the work is at night – seeing prisoners and seeing policemen. Many prisoners say that they have been beaten up and many policeman also say that they have been beaten up, so you have to go and see them both. We had to go out and see murders, rapes, all of it. I think that we were asked because of K.A.R.E.S. We already had a contact with the police because at accidents we met together, fire, police, ambulance, and ourselves. I suspect that was the reason why we were asked. We had a relationship with the police and so as a consequence we became the police surgeons when the other doctor retired. We were the obvious ones.

A police surgeon's job is firstly not a policeman and also not a surgeon. This was my spiel to every prisoner I used to go in and see. They looked at me as if to say, 'what the hell are you doing here?' and I would say 'I am not a policeman, I am not a surgeon, I am a GP and I come and see prisoners'. I had to say that because otherwise there was a presumption that I was on the police side, whereas one was not, one was independent. That was the most important thing to say. Quite often one met the same chaps. We did not have to attend post mortems, this went to the pathologists. Our work ended possibly with 'death suspicious and why', but it was then taken over by the pathologists. Suicides were not uncommon, unfortunately. With prisoners, we just examined them to see if they were fit to be detained, and the police to see if their injuries were consistent with being beaten up by the prisoners or vice versa. We had to record every injury. We had to spend some time in court, but not if one could avoid it. I used to hate it, it was not my scene. I think that it was a big mistake my being a police surgeon because it was totally foreign to my philosophy. When I retired, being the police surgeon was still going, but when Ian Nash retired, it went. It was he that had kept it going.

Unrelated to being police surgeons, Trish and I were once on our way back from a dance in Maidstone, and when we came to Hothfield there was a typical buzz and lights and police cars, so there had obviously been a crash. So I stopped and got out and there was a chap in a car who appeared to be unconscious. The car was off the road. So I got into his car and I was looking at him, the police were with me. I think that he was playing 'possum' actually because he had caused the accident. I ran my hands over him in the dark, he had his head back, and the whole of his hair went back – he had got a toupee! I thought he had been scalped. He was boozed but he got away with it actually, he was a local councillor, which was very upsetting to me. This incident was used by Mr Gorrell Barnes who used to write for Emergency Ward Ten. He was a film writer. He used to come and ask me questions sometimes: 'what would be the circumstances for so and so and what was the jargon'.

CHAPTER 16: RISKY AND ODD INCIDENTS

We were talking about guns earlier. We were always having trouble with dairymen. They changed their jobs as frequently as they changed their trousers just about. They were always moving because they thought that the next job was going to be better. I got called to one who was way up in Hastingleigh; the cowman there had discovered that his wife had been two-timing him and decided to threaten her with his shot gun. She ran off to the farmer and said,' look he is wanting to shoot me'. So I was rung up and I also rang the police and they said, 'we will send an officer with you, you had better liaise with him'. I said 'fine, you know where it is' and he said 'yes', and then he said, 'well, we will keep a low profile because as you know the chap well, we will expect you to do the negotiating'. I remember it was a weekend, a Saturday afternoon and the sun was shining. I went up to Hastingleigh, expecting a police car to be lurking about. I hung around a bit waiting for the police to arrive, giving the chap time to come from wherever he was. I went into the house and the fellow was there with his gun saying, 'what do you want'. I said, 'look, come on' and sat there chatting to him until he decided that he would come with me as a voluntary patient to St Augustine's because he had been showing symptoms before this. So I went out of the door with his gun in my hand which he had given to me and said, 'it's OK chaps' but there was nobody there at all. Then I heard a kind of 'pop, pop, pop' and it was the Bobby from Chilham on his little motor bike, arriving up the hill. I carried on and put the man in the car and took him to St Augustine's and he went in as a voluntary patient.

Another time, also in Hastingleigh, a chap was threatening his family with a sword and his wife phoned up. Despite the fact that we were about to go out to dinner, Trish came with me. Obviously the fellow had had too much to drink. I was there quite a long time and poor, old Trish was sitting in the car worrying about me. It was always when we were going out to dinner or already out. Anyway, he calmed down. I think the presence of someone outside the family often calms people down as long as they are not wearing a helmet. A helmet does, unfortunately, look as though they are in trouble. People react much better to somebody who is not authoritarian and. probably, who they know.

Another occasion was when we were out with Trish's parents celebrating a birthday or something, and I got a call to a country house in the village owned by an ex-army gentleman who commuted to London. His wife rang up and said he has gone out with a shot gun and they had heard two shots. City commuters in those days often went up to London on the 10 am train, got the 4 pm back having had a liquid lunch, and then had three gin and tonics in the restaurant car between Cannon Street and Ashford – so he had been in a state and had been angry when he went out with his shot gun. They had heard two shots and they thought he had done himself in. They had called and called and got no answer. I went with my car and drove along the track, and there in the middle of the road, in the headlights, was the gentleman concerned with his shot gun. I got out of the car and said who I was: 'hello, it is me – what is going on'. He said, 'I have been shooting ducks'. I said, 'it is a bit dark for that', because it was nearly nine o'clock at night in the winter. I said, 'look, you have worried everybody, your family are all worried thinking that you have gone and shot yourself and you have not'.. He said 'oh, ha, ha' and then I said, 'look, better let me have the gun' because initially he had been quite aggressive when the car lights came up and he had raised the gun at me when I had approached. So I took the gun from him and opened it having presumed that it would be empty after two shots had been fired, but it was still loaded! However, he went peacefully home and that was that. Then I went back and had supper at the Wife of Bath.

I think that it was important that I had a shot gun licence because I was able to confiscate or take guns into my care if somebody was posing a threat and that, funnily enough, happened with somebody on the College farm, once more a cowman, who was behaving very oddly and was becoming very difficult. His wife was frightened about him because he had a gun. So I remember talking to him and saying, 'look, for everybody's peace of mind etc'. When the crisis was over, I handed the gun back. A shot gun was, unfortunately, one of the ways of either shooting other people or themselves, and suicides with shotguns were not uncommon. Not pleasant.

As I said, I think, from my small experience in these things, that somebody who is not wearing a helmet and not official has far more chance of dealing with somebody who is threatening than someone who is. There was a chap who was sitting on a windowsill in Ashford saying he was going to jump out of a second floor flat. So the answer was to go and sit on the windowsill next door to him and talk to him. This happened, it was a police surgeon call, he was not a patient. I must say that the police kept out of the way. I do not think that he intended jumping anyway, he was just doing it because he was fed up with life and wife, that was all, but you never know which it is. I was not foolish enough to sit on the same windowsill as him; I was sitting on a windowsill of the next window.

I went with the police to another chap whose female next-door neighbour had rung up to complain that he had been going round with a hammer and he had threatened her and so forth. The heavy mob was called out to go and deal with him and they thought the police surgeon ought to go as well. So we went along to his flat in Bockhanger. The police were already there. There was a large sergeant, a chap with a big shield, a couple of others with a battering ram to break the door down, and myself. They called and called and he would not come and there was no sound at all. So number one policeman knocks the door down, number two went straight through and fell on the floor, the next one ran over him with his shield, and I followed. There was the gentleman in question, sitting at his kitchen table having a cup of tea, as calm as anything saying, 'what's up'. He had not answered the door because he could not be bothered.

There were also unforeseen, 'odd', incidents. For example, whilst a trainee at the Practice, when Mac was away, I had to cover. It seemed to me that I could be called for anything and everything. On this occasion at Whitsun, being a trainee I still had to work with a qualified locum doctor – William McGowan. A patient had died on the Whit Friday. It was a very, very hot weekend. He had been out gardening and he died. I went up to sort him out and the undertakers arrived and the family wanted the body to stay at home over the weekend. I was then rung up on Bank Holiday Monday by the Crematorium, because he was being cremated, to say that they were sorry I could not have Dr McGowan as the 'Part two' cremation doctor, since he was a partner. I said that he was not, he was a locum, but they said he is still working in the same practice as me and it would be illegal for him to sign the form. So on Bank Holiday Monday, I had to find a second doctor in a hurry to come out and sign the form because the funeral was quite soon, (in a quick slot), in Canterbury. So I managed to get a lady doctor who used to do locums, to come out. I must admit, she was always a doctor who kept well inside the law.

We met down in Wye and I took her up to the bungalow. It was an interesting sort of bungalow, you go in the front door and all the interior doors were half glazed, having got lightly frosted glass in them. We were ushered into the room where, on the trestles, was the coffin. I shut the door and said, 'well, there he is, he is in there.' She said, 'well I have got to see the body', and I said, 'well it is all screwed down'. Fortunately, the son of the deceased was a carpenter, so I went to see him to say, 'we just need to check on his body. Could I borrow a screwdriver?' A screwdriver was produced and I then learned that the screws of the coffin were covered with little screwed-in pegs. I had to undo six pegs – three on each side – and had to stand up on a chair to do this. All of this could vaguely be seen through the glass door.

Well, when I had unscrewed all these screws, what happened was, the lid 'pops up' as he had blown a bit. I said to the doctor, 'it does not look a bit like him now, but that is my patient,' and she said, 'all right, close it back up again, please.' But we had great difficulty in getting the lid back on. I got a screw in one end and could not get one in the other. In the end, I said, 'well, there is only one thing for it; you will have to sit on top of the coffin.' So she got the chair and did so, but I still had great difficulty in getting these screws in. I just could not screw them down and get the knobs on properly. So there was a gap left, as it would not completely close, which worried me.

So the next day, which was Tuesday, when the undertakers were going to collect him from the bungalow, I rang them up and said, 'look, I think that you have got to be very careful because...' and I explained what had happened. They just roared with laughter. I said, 'well it is all very funny for you people, but if you lifted it up by the lid, it might come off.'

They thought it was the funniest thing that had ever happened to them. It was rather a fraught weekend!

There was another occasion when a nurse and I, as the GP, had to go to deal with a male patient who had died. Whilst we were sorting out the patient, we noticed a set of false teeth on top of the chest of drawers and tried to get them into the deceased man's mouth. At that moment his wife, who had been waiting in the adjoining room, knocked on the door and asked to get her false teeth which were on top of the chest of drawers. The nurse resourcefully said that she would bring them to her and hastily closed the door. We had to rapidly remove the teeth, wash them and hand them over to his wife!

One sunny afternoon, I was minding my own business in the surgery, probably filling in accident forms or insurance forms as one had to do. The receptionist came through and said, 'there is a couple of young people who have come in and want to see you urgently doctor – they appear very upset.' So I said, 'well all right I will see them'. In they came and they were a couple of 17-year-olds whom I had known for a long time. The chap said, 'well, we think that we need to have the 'morning after pill', doctor.' I said 'yes, well fine and it depends of course on how long ago you had intercourse'. 'Oh, twenty minutes ago'. I tried hard not to laugh. I thought what a fantastic thing; I knew them both well and said, 'good on you'. Really that was great; it was that sort of day, it was lovely and they had been out enjoying it and could not have been too far from the surgery!

CHAPTER 17: FAMILY MOVE TO BILTING 1973

We moved out of Wye to Further Northfield, Bilting in 1973. Marianne was 14 when we moved, She had not wanted to move, she wanted to stay in the village – all her friends were there. So then we became a taxi service. Her friends did continue to call in.

One thing the previous owners had left behind was a top hat, which has proved most useful over the years.

I had always felt that I ought to be in the village but as time went on, it became apparent that the necessity was no longer there. Communications and transport were good and a larger number of the patients lived outside Wye. We had a surgery that was accessible in minutes. Even so, there was a certain amount of resentment when I did move out of the village which I

Below: Outside Further Northfield with our teenage children. Left to right: William, Marianne, Trish, Me, Caroline, Johnny

Top: Trish and I at a wedding, with me wearing the inherited top hat

Above: Further Northfield in the snow

Portrait of Canon Brade-Birks, Vicar of Godmersham

was aware of – people felt that I was no longer there. Rob Johnson was even further away in Brook. But it was the fact that I had always been there and they knew the door was there to knock on if necessary.

Canon Brade-Birks[xxii] was the vicar of Godmersham and Crundale for years and years. He had also lectured at the College and was made a Fellow. He had a double degree – he had a degree in science from Manchester, and he was a world authority on centipedes and millipedes. He was the vicar of Godmersham and Crundale for donkey's ages and he was a very good pastoral vicar – he knew everybody in the parish. We had hardly arrived at Godmersham before he appeared on the doorstep.

It was he who told us to call our house 'Further Northfield'. Because he was a man of many parts - he was also a local historian. Our house was called 'The Cottage' or no. 28 Bilting. Well there were other houses called The Cottage at the top of the lane and down the lane – a lot of Cottages. One problem was that at the time we were getting a lot of post and we could not afford for it to go missing. Canon Brade-Birks came one day, looked at the house and told us how old it was and a lot of things that we did not know. When we said that we wanted a name for it he said to me, 'when you have a half day, come down for tea'. So I went down to the vicarage for tea and he had all the maps of the area, tithe maps and goodness knows what laid out, because he kept them all. He was very astute. He kept all the stuff in the vicarage (which is now where Fiona Sunley lives) – that was the old vicarage or rectory. He went through the field maps indicating that 'that one is Four Acres, that one is Brick Field, this one is Middlefield.' Every field had a name, because otherwise how does a farmer know where to go, or to tell his chaps to go? It has to be, 'well you go to plough Middlefield tomorrow and on Friday we will do Lower Middlefield and Upper Middlefield'. There was one field called Northfield, and one called Further Northfield and our house is within Further Northfield. So that was it. He decreed it to be Further Northfield – so it was he who told us that this is what we should call it. I still have the letter of the details he sent and it was he who got Further Northfield 'listed'.

Canon Brade-Birks' services were renowned as being educational rather than ecclesiastical. They had a big following. One day we were minding our own business on a Sunday morning and had not been at the Church, when there was a knock on the door and there were the two Churchwardens and a doubled-up vicar who came in through our door with a strangulated hernia. So he literally

(4

The name of the field out of which land for this house was taken is called Further North Field and so I suggest for the name of the house, as appropriate, Northfield.

The land on which the house stands is part of one of the eight farms in Godmersham given in A.D. 824 by Beornulph King of the Mercians to Wulfred Archbishop of Canterbury and of one of the same eight farms mentioned more than 250 years later in the Domesday Book (1086). The Charter of 824 is in BM.

The map No 14 in the Survey of Kent by Andrews, Dury and Herbert, 1769, is not very satisfactory

(5

and the house is not clearly marked on it. But the map itself is interesting as showing the general layout of the local features and the course of the Roman road now superseded by the A28.

The house appears to have a core of early date – before 1625 – indicated by the use of "Tudor" bricks in the fireplace recently opened out. But there have been many changes in the structure especially in recent years. The open nature of the timber work on the front of the building suggests a date late in the period before 1625, perhaps in Elizabethan times or even later.

Yours sincerely
A. Graham Brade-Birks
Vicar of Godmersham

Letter from Canon Brade-Birks naming Further Northfield 1972

lay down in the house and with a bit of help I managed to push it back. He went off straight back to the Church and carried on with his service. That was the sort of man he was.

I had the good fortune of knowing him quite well because we used to go to the annual pre-session dinner and staff meeting at the College that the Principal held in September before the beginning of the new academic year. All the 'good and the great' from College went, including Brade-Birks. I would be invited because I was the College doctor. I used to take him when he was no longer mobile. He told me on one of these occasions that he had been to an international meeting of the Centipedes and Millipedes Society held in Manchester, which, I think, was his home town; he was there aged 85, as the Chairman. When it was all over, there were 'any questions' and a chap got up and said, 'well I now believe in reincarnation. I have been reading up articles by a Brade-Birks since I was a youngster, and I had presumed this gentleman would be dead – and here he is in front of me!'

He was an old man. He was losing his marbles a bit, but the villagers accepted this. His pastoral care was second to none – I often met him on the doorstep when someone was dying. When I arrived, there would be his moped, leaning by the door. At the end, rather against his own will, he went to a home for retired clergy – he had wanted to die in harness.

'BB' kept all the books of the Crundale library in the vicarage. This whole collection is very famous, dating from the 1600s, and was created by the Crundale vicar of that time. He obviously lent some of the books out as there was an inventory of 'books in, books out', which I have seen as it was in the Godmersham and Crundale Heritage Centre. 'BB' was frightened that when he went that they would all go to the Diocese of Canterbury. He made sure, though, that all of the book collection went to the College at Wye and not to Canterbury. He considered that they belonged to the parish of Crundale and should be preserved locally. They very nearly left the area when Imperial took the College over, but they then went to the Godmersham and Crundale Heritage Centre. One of the books is a first edition of William Harvey's Circulation of the Blood, which I had the pleasure of touching one day (with gloves on) and actually looking at it. It is only a tiny book from1616. William Harvey, of course, was born in Folkestone and the local hospital is named after him. Trish remembered that BB had his portrait painted by John Ward – a full-length portrait, commissioned by the College, and it hung on the back stairs of the Science Laboratories next door to Prof. Schwabe's office. It is a fine portrait, in the red robes of the DSc.There it was on the stairs out of sight. Though there was one time when it was unofficially moved from the stairs and hung at the back of Godmersham church, during one of its many festivals, with the help of the sons of the artist and the doctor. The doctor was given a severe reprimand by Prof. Schwabe!

It was got back from Imperial College and it went to the Godmersham and Crundale Heritage Centre on permanent loan. There was a lot of fighting – the politics were incredible – and the chap who got it back was John Sunley. I think that the Parish just has to pay the insurance for it, which is not cheap. They had tried to value it at some enormous sum. It is of no interest to anybody else but the village.

BB's wife, Hilda, was a doctor and had practised locally in Chilham. They were amicable but they did not live together. Hilda had rheumatism and the vicarage was cold and damp and next to the river and I think that, in those days, they thought the miasma of the river was too much for her. She lived in Canterbury. They lunched together on Sundays after services and they met socially. In fact, the only time I really met her was at Professor Wain's house at Hastingleigh. It was some social event. She drove and BB did not, and as she was going out she got her hand caught in the door of the car and tore it badly. Somebody came rushing in and called for me, so I took her down to the surgery and sewed her up, took her back again and she drove home, taking her husband with her! She was a charming lady. They ended up together in a Clerical Home for retired clergy somewhere in Suffolk.

CHAPTER 18: FURTHER PRACTICE DEVELOPMENT AND TRAINEES

After the war more people were going into general practice out of choice, many with much life experience. There was a new College set up – The Royal College of GPs. John Perry and I joined – we thought that this was the right thing to do. I believed that general practice was important, it was not a second tier occupation, whereas my partner before had considered himself to be a second class citizen. In medical school at St. Thomas's, the consultants looked down on the people who were going into general practice. They did not get jobs in the teaching hospitals, only the ones who were going to become consultants did. You joined the College as a Licentiate of the Royal College of General Practitioners (LRCGP). There came a time when the Royal College of GPs decided that they were going to have a Membership – you could take another exam later. Then suddenly, they said, 'ah, we are going to have an exam; but for those of you who are already Licentiates, if you pay £50 now, you do not have to take it. Well, John Perry and I looked at each other when this information came, and said, 'We cannot afford that,' – £50 was school fees for a term then. We were screwed, we absolutely could not afford it, and so we said no.

Years later, I went up to be vetted to see if I should continue as a GP trainer. I went in front of a Board. I remember that it was an appalling set-up. Rob Johnson and I went together. We said that if we were going to take on trainees, as a two doctor practice, we both had to be responsible for the trainees. So up we went, and we were both interviewed. We had to go to Maidstone to Preston Hall, the old Chest Hospital, just outside the town. We had asked for appointments at the beginning and end of the session so we could cover for one-another, but they gave us consecutive times so we had to get a locum. We arrived there and the waiting room was the gentlemen's loo, which was outside the Board Room. I must say, I took umbrage and said I am not going to wait there and went downstairs to wait. I thought it was not on and they could come down and collect me. Well, when I got in front of this panel, I think there were eight of them, and they did the usual questions, 'what were your attitudes' and so on. They asked, 'why have you not got a Membership?' Looking at the list of panel members, I saw that there were three GPs that I knew had bought theirs. So I said, 'you see, at the time, I could not afford to buy it like some of you' and three heads went down and studied their papers intently. Rob was interviewed as well – he was a bit headstrong. I knew that if we both did not get the job together we could not do it. The end result of it was that they offered me the job of supervising trainees, but not him. So I turned it down. I never took on the Membership. Trish says that I came back incensed saying, 'How dare they – none of them have a clue about general practice.' You know your colleagues – there were some GPs on the panel who, somehow over

Preston Hall, the old Chest Hospital

the years, had not become exactly enthusiastic about general practice. Then not long after that there was a trainee who had been appointed to a practice in Ashford. Unfortunately, the trainer went sick, so they had not got a trainer for him. Rob had left by then and they made me trainer.

When there were three partners and one left the practice it might take six months to find someone new. This meant that with one less, of course, we shared the pot, and that managed to pay off our debts. Then when number three joined us, it went back again and so did the pay. This happened two or three times. There was supposed to be a ratio of doctor to patient of something like 2,000 or perhaps 1,500 in a rural area, I am not sure. On the other hand with four of us we had eight and a half thousand patients at one time. The numbers grew steadily because of the way building went on and also for the fact that we hung on to our patients. People do not move very far away when they live in the country, they move about 10 or 15 miles. If somebody gets married the surgery takes on the husband and then eventually children and perhaps mother-in-law. This went on everywhere. We reckoned actually that the practice was a hundred square miles – if you think that Wye was in the centre with the roads going out, be it up to Waltham over to Brabourne, over to Sellinge, over to Mersham, over to Aldington, into Ashford. We did not go the other side of Ashford, nor have anybody in Charing but Challock yes, Molash yes, Chilham yes, Boughton Aluph, Bossingham, Lower Hardes. If you work it out you will find that all these are at a 5 mile radius from Wye, – approximately 10 by 10. You did find that the odd people did move that bit further and they used to say 'you will hang on to us won't you doctor?' and one hoped that they wouldn't fall ill. Getting back to the practice, when Rob left, Ian Nash and I had a very hard time for a couple of years. I think that possibly we had Amanda then for a short while.

After two years we took on a new partner. Unfortunately, as sometimes happens in any partnerships, views and attitudes clashed, causing a lot of disharmony within the practice. References provided had been glowing, reasons given for leaving had been robust and former partners were sorry about their departure. This happened before the practice moved into Oxenturn Road. There were then the three of us for just a few years. We first realised something was wrong when about five patients of mine, whom I had known for years, suddenly rang to say 'why did you take me off your list, Gerry?' People were very upset. 'Why did I take them off the list?' We had not realised what was happening. If patients who lived on Stone Street or in Ashford, for example, had requested a home visit, we discovered that they had been taken off the list, based on the fact that they lived too far away. These decisions about patients were being made without Ian's or my knowledge by the new partner. It happened largely when I was on holiday.

Then we took on Roz Waller as an assistant with a view to partnership. Ian and I felt that it was important that we had a woman in the practice, very important, but our new partner was strongly opposed to the idea and it was difficult for all of us, particularly Roz, although she had Ian's and my support. This happened during the preparation for the move from Little Chequers to Oxenturn Road and there were four of us trying to work in a two-consulting-room practice, which was not easy. That was a bad time, it was very difficult. Medicine is easy but it is these sorts of things that are difficult.

As it turned out, the partner eventually went off on sick leave relating to a chronic pain condition and the disharmony was resolved without need for any action on either part. We were notified that, during the time off for sick leave, he was working for more than one organisation. We had a policy that any money that you earned in surgery time - for example, if you let somebody go off for a police service job, or give lectures in surgery time - the money went into the kitty, but throughout this time the practice received no financial remuneration. In the end it all piled up and in time he retired on medical grounds with pension and everything.

Rob Johnson, Ian Nash, and I were together for some time. When Rob left, Ian and I had been on our own for a bit and found it rather difficult to find anybody. It was a terrific strain, actually. Of course trainees came in. The first trainee was Jolyon Miles and he stayed on. We had about six trainees all together. At that time they did six months with us, then went to the hospital for two years, then came back for six months – three years in total. But in the meantime, whilst at the hospital, we still saw them – more socially than professionally. It was not at all expected that they would join our practice; in fact it was the thing not to in a way, although Jolyon did. We had a husband and wife as trainees – she was part-time. They went down to the West Country somewhere. We had another who is principal doctor now at the Willesborough Practice. There was another, tall and thin, now the principal doctor in Deal. They all worked out well; they were all very good.

David M. had joined the practice and was with us for a time. He was a live wire and was good. He was a computer whizz, which I never was, but if I was in trouble, I went to him. We did get ourselves computer literate at the surgery. We were hoping he would become a partner and that he would computerise the Practice.

The interaction with trainees was very much that they were allowed to do as much as they felt capable of doing. On the other hand, we were totally responsibility for them. The most important thing that they needed, I found, was to be sure that you were available. If they had a problem, they could just ring you up. The people who were administrating the trainee scheme had once been in general practice but were beginning to lose touch, as they were trying to implement ideas with very little real inside knowledge about current practice. They came under the NHS and were GP orientated, but they had become administrators. They were responsible for seeing that we did our so many hours ongoing training requirement and had to send our bits of paper in to say that we had been present at this lecture etc to meet the conditions. It was the beginning of increased bureaucracy, which was fair enough because it was good, but like all these things the learning was always at night because one was presumed to be around 24 hours a day.

I was invited to join the odd committee – one was called Cogwheel, which was supposed to integrate the hospital and general practices. It has died in the morass of time. Meetings were once a month and they were morning sessions. They had to be during the day, of course, because it was administrators who were running them. So one had to finish a surgery and belt up to somewhere in Thanet. At that time I think that Canterbury certainly had the greater influence. It was trying at that time, as I said, to become a part of the new university and they had established the post-graduate centre at the hospital which we went to for a lecture each week on Tuesdays in the afternoon. It was definitely trying to 'pull' so I went to these Cogwheel meetings but it was all about administration which was not my scene at all. They were about how they were going to do this and that. We went to a different place each month and there was an office for the administrator in every place, which cannot have been used much – carpeted and all the rest of it – that did not help one's views much.

Trish reminded me that we had a friend who was a senior partner who practised in Ashford. We had been great sailing friends. He was an official GP trainer. He was in charge and took it very, very seriously. I went over one day to see his methods of teaching and he had installed in the wall of the surgery a mirror. It was a two way mirror. So somebody could be the other side of the mirror and watch what was going on – i.e. the consultation between the trainee and the patient. This was like a red rag to a bull to me. I believed it to be a breach of confidentiality. The patients were supposed to know that they were going to be observed and supposed to agree to it. It did strike me as pushing the limits a bit. I was horrified. We used to do role play and video sessions. But there is a difference between that and examining somebody.

There were training courses run all over the place, one could go on a week's course. I went on a residential course in Westcliffe on Sea once. I must say I was an older one amongst the young, and it was the jargon I could not handle. It was the beginning of jargonese coming in a big way. The sort of thing that got me was something about 'group intercourse'. I said that as far as I was concerned I presumed that this was a 'gang bang', and this went down like a lead balloon. At the end of the course they said what were your views on the course and I said that I had learnt an awful lot on the course about jargon which I had been unaware of. Nowadays this training is called Continuous Professional Development (CPD) which, or course, is good.

I really came unstuck as well when the Deanery came round to inspect the practice to see if it was fit for trainees to be trained. The trainee was to be interviewed in the morning, and I was going to be interviewed in the afternoon. There was a group of about six people – three from elsewhere and three locals. So I sorted the day out so that I had not got anything to do in the afternoon. The trainee came in after lunch, and he was really very poorly, he had got the most terrible cold and sinusitis, he felt awful. The meeting was scheduled for 2.30 pm. By 3.30 pm nobody had turned up so I said to him, I will sort this out, you have done your bit this morning – go home. So off he went home. The inspection group did not turn up until 5 pm. They had got behind with another practice that they had been to, hence their lateness. By that time I was not best pleased and they nit-picked around the place and pulled out notes and looked at them and questioned me and said well, 'how do you assess your trainees'. I said, 'well, we discuss them amongst ourselves, with the practice staff and with the cleaners'. Their reaction was – 'What!' I did not say this deliberately, it was just that was what we did because they were two good, super cleaners and they would say, 'oh, he's getting on all right', because it was the way that they were treated by them. This was all part of the practice, it was important to us – you had to get an idea of what they were like because if they were rude to cleaners, they would be rude to patients.

This was the trouble training in the hospitals. We were still responsible for training and if there was trouble for trainees with hospital training they should have come to us. We had one spat, which was a good spat actually. One of the trainees was a barrack room lawyer – he knew what he wanted and he found that the hospitals were not obeying the contracts that they had got for their 2-year hospital stints. There were all kinds of things going on which should not have been, which would have been normal twenty years before, but were, at that time, changed within hospitals. These were that they did not have to cover for colleagues in other specialities. They did their own job and if they were off, they were off, and when they were on they were on. They were being dictated to that they should cover for so and so when they were on leave. This particular trainee did not agree with this and pointed it out to the management. He wrote this down in a letter, absolutely word for word. He brought the letter to me to check before sending it off, which was good of him. I looked at it and said, 'well I think that you could water that down a bit'. It was pretty harsh. It went in and the next day I was phoned up by the Chief Medical Officer, who was a friend of mine. He said, 'what is this all about?' and I said, 'yes – it was much worse when it was first composed'. Anyhow, he had got them because what he stated was correct. That was it. They had been getting away with it for years. So they treated him carefully and we got a bit of a reputation.

Another amusing thing was with another trainee. He went round to see somebody called Spitfire J., a lady of renown in the village. She really did speak her mind without any qualms. A very tough character but very straightforward, a villager married to Jock J., who had a pretty hard time. He was always out with his dog sitting on the wall. She was really fine, underneath it all. I saw a lot of her because Jock was ill for a long time, and so on and then he died and I saw about that. Then one day she was poorly and I said to the trainee, 'Well, pop round and see her. She will be pretty dodgy with you and probably be quite rude,' I forewarned him.' He came back with his tail between his legs saying that she had told him to 'b......off' and 'what has happened to that chap, Flack?' – which was as I expected. So I said, 'Well, we will go back later. He said, 'Well I bet you that she will not be like that to you,' and I said, 'Well I bet she is. I bet you five shillings that when I go to the door, she will swear at me.' So we went along and at the door she said, 'Where the b......hell have you been? Why did you not coming instead of sending.......?' So I said to the trainee, 'five bob' and that shut her up immediately and she said 'what's that for?' And I said, 'because I bet him five shillings that you would swear at me when I came.' She used to leave a bottle of cherry brandy on the doorstep every Christmas; home-made cherry brandy. She lived in Bridge Street.

Miss J was from Boughton Aluph, a spinster and a tough cookie – one of my real heroines. She was an agricultural adviser on hop culture, working for ADAS, and a staunch feminist and environmentalist. She developed ovarian cancer and I saw a lot of her. In those days we treated this at home. I used to tap her tummy fluid – monthly and later fortnightly, then weekly. (All the implements for this were at the surgery, left by previous doctors. One ex-locum had left all his implements including dental tools.) In the end, in September, Miss J said, 'I'd like to go and see some of my old farms.' I took her to three farms in the area. It was like taking royalty! One hop garden was down after some gales and she said to the farmer, 'I told you to use such and such gauge wire!' She was the first case I knew to have bequeathed her corneas at her death. So I had to ring the West Kent eye hospital immediately to have her corneas removed in the middle of the night by a surgeon.

As well as Wye College and ADAS, there was an Artificial Insemination unit locally, which had a phone number very similar to our own. Quite often I would get a phone call in a rural accent: 'Could you come to X Farm. Our Buttercup's bulling now!'

It was in 1979 that Trish and I celebrated our Silver Wedding Anniversary. Later that day we travelled to Buckingham Palace to a Royal Garden Party.

Above: Silver Wedding at Further Northfield

Right: Attending Buckingham Palace Garden Party on our Silver Wedding Day

CHAPTER 19: THE SHOOTING

I am happy to talk about the shooting; it is a thing of the past. What people may not know is that we had ten years of being stalked prior to this, by this chap. In fact, the shooting was quite a relief as it was the absolute end of it. As time has gone by, one has forgotten how many incidents this gentleman created against the practice and so many other people in the area, in so many ways. And the sadness is, of course, that he was a clever man, but I guess he would be regarded as a psychopath.

We were certainly not alone in his verbal and written attacks; when he was a small boy he was difficult and harassed other school kids, especially the girls. Trish knew two girls who used to work in the Co-op. When they used to go to Bodsham School, apparently Leslie Smith harassed them dreadfully and would not leave them alone. This then continued on the bus when they went to Ashford School.

The thing is he was most extraordinarily clever. He upset a lot of people all around the place. Hastingleigh is a fantastic village; I often used to say to Trish that if I did not live where we do, I would rather live in Hastingleigh than anywhere because the community was so good. It is a community that looks after its own. If anybody up there was ill or had mental problems I never had to send a district nurse, unless it was something really serious, because they looked after each other. People who had been ex-nurses and so on looked after others. Because of the hill, they were isolated a bit in the bad weather, so they looked after themselves. They were a group apart. They put up with him, with this chap.

The parents were local, the Smiths. His mother had been a school teacher, his father was absolutely a straight guy, but was dominated by his wife, and Leslie ran rings round both of them. They were getting on in age when they had him. Even as a small boy, I remember him from aged about six or seven and he was always a very difficult little chap. As he got older and became a teenager, he was worse. He was dominant in the house and treated his parents appallingly. He was an only child. He was clever - he went to grammar school and went to college. He had a definite artistic bent - I always remember there was a sign outside the New Flying Horse pub, of the Pegasus. He painted that. He was quite an accomplished builder. He could turn his hand to most things. Ian Nash had his kitchen completely re-fitted by him and also had his swimming pool built by him. He seemed to have collected a group of followers because various of his incidents required more than himself.

He got to know the practice quite well and odd things started to occur. Other than his work, he obviously had other things going on which were underhand and which people did not know about. His mother went ill and was looked after at home. There came a time when she went into hospital. She was in hospital for probably about six weeks, which is a long time to be in hospital. He was there every day meticulously taking notes about everything. When she died, obviously he then turned it on the hospital and the practice. Trish reminded me that his mother had in the past had pneumonia two or three winters running and I had looked after her at home. During her final illness I do not know why, perhaps I had a big surgery, so a colleague went up to see her and Leslie Smith resented it. 'Where's Flack?' Flack had not turned up, so from that moment on – I was in the wrong. But when his mother was in hospital, he still used to phone me up to tell me what was going on and I used to say why they were doing this, that and the other. But little did I know that he was festering and noting everything in detail at the hospital. Trish thought he made a nuisance of himself when he was on the medical ward and they decided in the end that they would send her to intensive care – she needed specialist help so they decided to give her care where she got one to one treatment. He was satisfied with that because he had been complaining that she was not getting the right treatment. In the end, he formally complained about the Wye practice and the hospital but the complaint was thrown out. He tried to sue the hospital but left it too late and was 'out of time'. He lodged a complaint against the surgery and we were willing to be investigated, but events took over before this happened.

That was when the problem began against the practice and Ian and I were the two who were obviously involved. I think the first time that I ever knew about it was one day I was on call for the weekend. I came out to the car and under my windscreen wiper was a notice saying 'an eye for an eye and a tooth for a tooth'. I thought, 'what on earth is this?' I carried on to the surgery, got to the surgery and thought, 'that's funny'. All over the village there were stickers, including a whole lot stuck on the windows of the surgery saying 'doctors do not care about old people' and a poem/jingle naming Ian Nash and myself. That was the start and we guessed it was him because it was very professionally done. He was a good artist and it was very clever stuff – if you were not on the other side of it, it was quite amusing. The stickers were on all the car parks around, up the walls at Withersdane, the College, and other villages around. He had obviously got a little team going as well, because he had a little close knit coven of friends who were all anti-establishment. That was part of it, but then other things happened, including cartoons with captions. The surgery was broken into and poor Ian's brake cables were cut in his car. He went down the hill and nearly straight across the crossing. We got the police involved

Cartoon harassment by Smith

right from the word go but they seemed to be unable to pin anything on him.

A lot of it is surmise and guesswork. It is awfully difficult to explain but he obviously had some influence and people were scared of him and of what he could do. This was one of the things all the way through because if anybody turned against him, something happened to them and nobody could prove it. Somebody, for example, made a comment about him, and they found that their cat was killed. That was one of the things. Another thing, a chap who lived opposite him, objected to him doing something or other and there was paint all over his car. It was these sort of little things; everybody knew, but the police could never prove anything because it was all circumstantial. No one saw him do it. There was a lady in Hastingleigh who crossed him, I do not know quite how. She was a widow, literally just widowed, and within a week of the funeral she had pornographic literature put through her letterbox. She first of all got phone calls and then literature through the door – this was stuff from Scandinavia. He was caught phone tapping on someone else and went to gaol. He had a little van that looked like a telephone van. Funnily enough he sent me a tape of the phone tapping and I still have it. He had a printing press and printed everything out but the police could never find it. We believed that it was buried in the wood somewhere. Poor chap, he spent so much time doing this.

Dr. G. S. Flack,
M.B., B.S., D.Obst.R.C.O.G.

Dr. I. T. Nash,
M.B., B.S.

The Surgery,
Little Chequers,
Wye,
Ashford,
Kent. TN25 5DX
Tel: Wye (0233) 812414

The Editor
International Daily News
Via Barberia 3 00187
Rome
Italy

23rd April 1989

Dear Sir,

I was enthralled reading the SATANIC VERSES by SALMAN RUSHTE, to discover the perception, anlytical sensitivity and personal courage of the author,
SALMAN RUSHTE is a deeply committed religious philosopher who has brought new hope to the wasteland of entrenched esoteric dogma and ossified teachings of the KORAN.
The deluded purblind adherants to this false doctrine have become manipulated dupes of the cynical self seeking political demagogs in Teheran.
An inspired prophet has risen like the Sphinx, from the conflagration of revolution in Iran, to lead the Islamic peoples out of the dark ages of religious corruption, into the twentieth century and an awakening to truth and enlightenment.
SALMAN RUSHTE may well prove to be the Messiah the Islamic world has prayed for so long in bondage to the tyranny of the Mullah's.
A Mahdi, the new Mohomet, has come from the barren wilderness of unreason to lead a Jehad of intellect and learning, against the fortresses of ignorance and reactionary orthodoxy which is the Islamic faith today,

Yours Sincerely,

Dr Gerrald Staunton Flack
M.B.,B.S.,Dr.Obst.R.C.O.G.

Forged letter circulated to the media and Arab vice Consuls by Smith

One of the things I got every other Tuesday was a brown envelope with death threats. It was a black card saying R.I.P. Dr. Gerald S. Flack 1929 – the date. My birth 28 April 1929 . . . I still have one of them. These arrived by mail to the house and you did not know where it came from. Trish thought that they were typed on an old-fashioned typewriter where the letters were not always in line. They were obviously all from the same typewriter. Eventually I lost patience with this and one day I took it to the surgery and said, 'look I have got another one in'. I wrote on it, return to sender Leslie Smith and his name and address in red. I had just had enough. Another time we found a hangman's noose hanging outside the surgery from the surgery door. When the girls turned up in the morning, they got there before us at 8 am, there was the hangman's noose.

Then came the big one. This was on a day at the time of the Fatwa on Salman Rushdie. Out of the blue I got a letter. It was tearing me off a strip. It was from a chap who was the Vice Consul in Bahrain or something, or the Arab Emirates accusing me of the most horrendous thing, saying that I was supposed to have written a letter to all the Arab newspapers saying that I was supportive of Salman Rushdie. It had been sent to newspapers all over the world, Australia, Canada, USA, South Africa, Ireland, everywhere you could think of he had sent these letters. This meant that the Fatwa might also apply to me. If only Leslie could have used his brain in a different way. About the same time I got two letters, one from The Times and one from The Telegraph saying, 'thank you for your communication, we will be in touch.' I had not sent anything. That really got me. I then rang The Observer saying, 'what is this all about?' and they read the letter to me. I said, 'if you print this, I shall sue you.' I contacted The Times and The Telegraph and they sent me the letter; that is how I found out. I rang up The Observer and said again, 'What is this all about? There is no way I have written you a letter and I want a copy of it.' Back it came and there was the letter that I was supposed to have written.

Fortunately for me, down the road from here was Vincent Hanna, who was Lord Gerry Fitt's son-in-law. Lord Fitt had been MP for West Belfast in Ireland during the troubles, and I saw him quite often. He and his family had been targeted by the IRA and he had even had a gunman come into his bedroom in the middle of the night. We were talking one day after he had had a heart attack and I mentioned that I was being pursued by Lesley Smith and wondered if I should move. 'Much better to stay put where you've got family support,' he said. 'If he's going to get you he will be even more determined if you move.'

Vincent Hanna was on the sharp end of using e-mails and all the rest of it and knew how to contact people. I went to him and said, 'what shall I do?' and he said, 'I will do it for you.' And he sat down and went through the night writing to all the editors of all the papers, and he sent this message to everyone, saying anyone who prints this will be sued. I had done the same to The Times and The Telegraph and said, 'look this is not me' and they sent me back the copies straight away. It still appeared in the Irish Times, however, but fortunately it died a natural death; but might not have done. It was a devious mind and very clever thing to do. The surgery staff all knew about this. They kept it to themselves, but they were quite worried about safety because in the village, the College has a lot of Muslim people there.

There was an incident about that time when Will and Kate came over for lunch. I think at the time they were living at Horsemonden. I said to Will – 'right, we will go up to the Compasses for a beer'. We went up on our own. The Compasses was very quiet though there were others in the bar. It was a lovely sunny day and we had half an hour to have a beer as it is our local. There at the other end of the bar, clad in a pair of shorts and polo shirt, is Leslie Smith. I am at one end and he is at the other. He started singing some song about hating Gerry Flack and so on and it was a lovely day so I said, 'Come on Leslie, do you not think it is time that this all stopped'. He picked up a glass and went for me. I ducked and it just took a piece of my tooth off. You can guess various locals were up there and they picked him up and bundled him out. Good old Essex John said, 'Do you want to get the police?' I said, 'no'. Just think about it – it would have been in the papers. 'Doctor assaulted in pub' – which is what he always hoped because he would have loved to get the publicity against me. He got it in the end because what happened was that he became difficult. He went to gaol for a while because of the phone tapping. He got caught and he was inside, so he had his gun licence taken away. This was very important to him – guns are power. Hastingleigh, being the village it was, got a bit frightened.

There was an old milk lady, Lorna Smith, up there and a girl who had had emotional problems and was not one hundred per cent recovered. He had taken up with her, much to the annoyance and anger of her family who were worried sick about her. She was old enough but was very, very vulnerable and he had 'taken her under his wing'. Lorna the milk lady had seen her car there at his house at night and obviously told her parents and they reacted. A few days later Leslie was seen sharpening a knife in a garage where his mates were and next day, poor Lorna came out of her house and all her tyres were slashed. Everyone knew who had done it but no one had seen him do it and could not prove it. Except there was a note on the windscreen saying, 'next time it will be your throat'. This was his pattern. What happened then was the village was getting increasingly concerned because his behaviour was getting more and more erratic. One day, just to annoy them, he went around with some air rifles in his van for all to see (air rifles are not illegal). So the village got very

Kentish Express, Thursday, May 19, 1988 3

Builder hounded GPs

AFTER the Hungerford massacre, villagers in Hastingleigh became concerned about a local builder, whom they said, was aggressive and drank a lot and who held a shotgun certificate.

'NO GUNS' RULE AFTER VILLAGE KEPT IN FEAR

No one would actually come forward and put their names to a statement, except Wye GP Dr Gerald Flack, who told Canterbury Crown Court on Monday of his anxiety.

After hearing of a campaign that Leslie Smith, 43, mounted against the Wye doctors, and of his non co-operation with police, Judge Paul Batterbury dismissed Smith's appeal against the withdrawal of his shotgun licence.

Smith, of Hawksdene Cottage, Hastingleigh, was ordered to pay £158 costs.

The court heard that Smith mounted a campaign against the doctors in Wye — mostly defamatory cartoons about them — and became very irrational following the death of his mother four years ago.

That time his shotgun licence was revoked, but Smith got it back again a year later, said Caroline Streets, for the Chief Constable.

Then, when his father died last year, local villagers became afraid that Smith, a bachelor who had a reputation for drinking, might again become irrational.

Dr Flack, who said he had known Smith for 30 years, told the court in evidence that he had been approached by local people who felt threatened by Smith's behaviour and feared that if he had a shotgun something might happen. Their fears were heightened by the recent Hungerford shootings.

The doctor said he acted because Smith fitted the medical category of being at risk.

"I felt initially that it was not my place to do anything," he went on, "but people who approached me would not make statements and I felt then I did not have much alternative."

After Smith's mother died in 1984 Smith had blamed him, said the doctor. He distributed defamatory cartoon leaflets and made threats and was drinking heavily.

In the last year incidents included a hangman's noose over the surgery door and 10 threatening letters, which Dr Flack believed had come from Smith. The court ruled that there was no evidence Smith was responsible. Smith had finally been struck off the doctor's list when he wanted him to treat a pet dog.

Several police officers gave evidence of Smith telling them to leave his property and described him as unco-operative and aggressive.

In his evidence Smith agreed that after his mother's death he had been very distressed, disturbed and drinking heavily for two years. He admitted that he had drawn the cartoons ridiculing the doctors.

However, his father's death had not affected him so seriously, he said, and he had now given up drinking altogether.

He denied sending Dr Flack threatening cards through the post and said he did not know of any villagers who thought him a potential danger.

Newspaper report of withdrawl of gun licence from Smith

concerned that he was going to get his gun back. It so happened that he applied to get them back. We were just about to go on holiday and someone came down from Hastingleigh to say they were terribly worried in the village that he was going to get them back and what could I do about it as none of them dared to sign things because of the consequences.

If you make a statement about why he should not be fit to have a gun licence, this goes to the defence and Leslie would read it and know exactly who sent it. I knew that this was trouble, but I just wrote, 'in my opinion Leslie Smith is unfit to have a shotgun or rifle, he could be a danger to others and to himself.' So that was it, I wrote the statement out and signed it. It was on a Saturday morning of the week we were going away. I knew it would cause problems. It went through various courts and ended up at Canterbury at the Assizes – a proper court, where there was a judge. I was the only witness. The police also opposed it. However, I was there and he had got me in Court, at last. Then I was in one box and he was in another. He had a defence solicitor, who then had a go at me. He questioned me saying, 'and did you send this letter to my client?' This was the 'return to sender letter' I had sent perhaps a year before. I said, 'I did'. The Judge said again, 'Did you?' and I said, 'Yes, I did'. He said, 'why did you send it?' I said: 'Well the index of suspicion was pretty high as to where it had come from your Honour'. He said, 'Well why do you think that?' and I said, 'Well previous episodes have led me to believe that this is where it had come from'. Then I said, 'Well, I had other occurrences'. 'What were they?' said the Judge. It did so happen that I had got all of the stuff in my bag with me and I produced it. Leslie then hung himself by wanting to show how clever he was having done all this and what he had sent off and so on, and so forth. He therefore admitted his guilt, but there was no law of harassment then. Of course, he did not get his licence. But he had had his day in Court to show how clever he was. But one realised then that things had changed. Time went on and I met him the odd time and he just passed by. Trish remembered his glaring, staring eyes which were quite unnerving. We have all the paper cuttings and a video of the news story on Southern Television. Not getting his gun licence was the last straw as far as he was concerned.

After that, you see, I was not alone, there was a police sergeant whom I knew well who had crossed him and he went and stood at the bus stop where his kids got off. This sort of thing. This is what he did. There were other people who did not dare say anything. People would come to me and tell me. There were so many people that he terrorised. You cannot imagine it. The last thing was that the police, eventually, had to take some action. There were no Wye police then, they were all Ashford. One became depressed and gave up on the police in the end.

One day, something happened that changed everything as far as I could tell; he was found on top of Hastingleigh hill in his car, a green Fiat, by a policeman and a police woman in a police car. The police woman got out, the policeman stayed in the car. She looked through the window and Leslie was in the car. He had apparently that night been into the pub at Hastingleigh, the Bowl – and had broken in. He was getting very short of cash because nobody would give him any work, particularly after the Court case. Everybody shunned him when they realised that he was a problem. Financially he accused me of losing him £100,000 per year and all his contracts etc. He had stolen some food from the pub. He had a slate up there and cleaned it of his name, so everyone knew that it must have been him who had gone in there. When the policewoman got to him, he threatened her with a knife and drove off at a rate of knots with the police car chasing him, but he just disappeared. So he was on the run from the police for a couple of weeks. It was extraordinary how their attitude changed when one of their own was threatened with a knife. He was sighted during those two weeks by different people. He was a local lad, he knew the place backwards, he knew everywhere. I think he thought of himself as a kind of terrorist cum backwoodsman, guerrilla fighter kind of thing and I think that he had a little gang of chaps who were on his side. In fact I know he had. They felt sorry for him.

During that two weeks I got a call one day by the police to go to a car in the woods up at Challock, with a body in it. A green car and as I knew that he had a green Fiat. I thought, perhaps it was Leslie. I went up there and it was not him, it was a chap from London whose wife had left him because of mortgage problems and there was a little note. Shortly after this, I had a flu-like illness and had been off work all week. I felt well enough to go back to work on the Friday. I came out of the house and the dog was behaving a bit oddly. I went down the garden, which was a daily routine as we had chickens, and thought, 'that's funny, there is a hole in the hedge and fence. I thought perhaps a tractor had done it because it was the farmer's field the other side. The dog looked at it. It was big enough for a man to get through, so I mended it and came back inside. I got in my car and drove round the block at 25 minutes past eight to be at the surgery by half past eight. Trish was staying at home with her father who was blind. I got to the top of the lane and as always could not get onto the main road, it was that time of day. I looked in the mirror and saw a green car right behind me. Leslie Smith got out and fired two shots with a revolver. I thought – oh he is just trying to frighten me. Then he came round to the side of the car and shot through the glass. Trish said that when I am embarrassed, I always put my hand up to my face. Either the glass deflected it or he did not see into the car. The bullet went straight through my arm and out again. The glass shattered, the extraordinary thing was that I did not realise until later.

Three shots had been fired and I knew that there were another three, so I threw myself down into the bottom of the car on the passenger side, and lay there with my head under the glove compartment, waiting for the next shot. All I heard then was a car go past. I could not see because the glass was shattered, but had not fallen out. As I was lying there, there beside me on the floor was the bullet, literally lying in my blood. After he had driven past, Roz Field drove past as well going to work. I did not get up because I was too frightened and just lay there for a few minutes. She did not see me just drove past because I was tucked up right against the hedge as one does turning left. I got out of the car and went to the house there – they were wonderful; they were great. The house was called the 'Crack of Dawn Cottages' and there was a young couple there. She was in the bath and he was about. He had heard the shots and came downstairs to have a look and I met them at the gate, as it were and said, 'better ring up Trish.' And I rang Trish first to say, 'Look, Leslie Smith has just shot me.' In fact this was a great relief. I did actually ring up the surgery. We had a radio telephone then and I rang up and said, 'look, I have been shot' but they did not think it was me because they did not know that I was coming back to work. They thought it was Jolyon, and the ambulance went to the wrong place at first.

In hospital after being shot

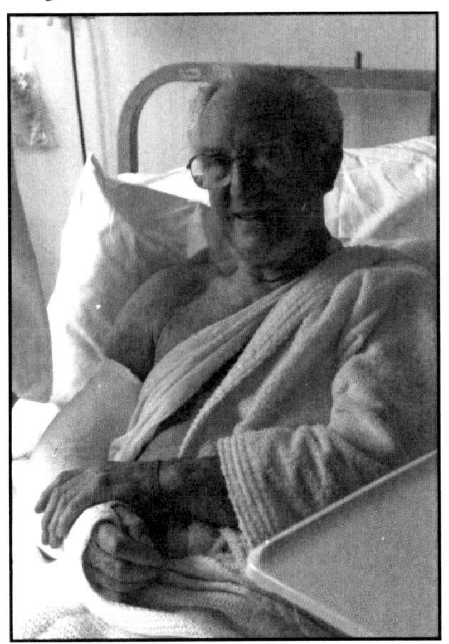

We later learned that Leslie had hidden behind the hedge and fence each morning waiting for me to go to work. I

Being interviewed by the Press outside the hospital

had been off work ill so he must have been there several mornings as I always left home regularly at 20 or 25 past eight, got in my car, drove round the loop and then on to Wye. It was pre-meditated and he obviously enjoyed this - it was part of the power buzz. At the trial he threatened both the judge and the prosecuting counsel which was not a good move on his part. The prosecuting counsel became a judge in Kent somewhere; his name is Nash and by chance I have met him once or twice since. Leslie was charged with attempted murder and found guilty, subject to psychiatric reports. He then tried to get off on various excuses and we had to go back to court again, first in Maidstone and secondly in Queen's Chambers in London, so sentencing was delayed; he was finally sentenced at the Old Bailey. We had to go to Court three times. He was sectioned, but I do not know when, he could have been sectioned from prison. He is now in Broadmoor. Trish wondered if Leslie Smith, being very clever, could wheedle his way around people whilst there. It has been hard to think that someone hates you enough to want to shoot you. That was rather destroying and I found it hard to cope with.

As Trish said, I have the habit of putting my arm up against my face when I feel embarrassed and it is a miracle that I did, because seeing the holes in my arm at the time I must say I thought, from an anatomical point of view, that my right arm had had it and would have been paralysed because the nerves and both bones are there and because I could not do anything with my hand to start with. But the bullet went between the two bones; it did break them both but probably because of the vibration rather than hitting them. It also

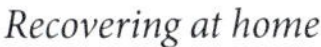

Recovering at home

missed the nerves and I had a full recovery. Quite amazing. It is really almost miraculous. Presumably he could not see me through the window because it was tessellated. It did not look like that in the various forensic pictures because, as I got out of the car, the whole window fell out, so obviously after he shot me, he could not see me, hopped in his car and buzzed off. If he had gone round to the front he would not have seen me either because I was lying in the well of the car. The presumption was that as the bullets there were quite big things, not .22s, they were .45 Smith & Wesson, but the premeditation was such that it was a First World War gun that he even had had to make the bullets for. You cannot buy them any more so he had to make his own. He had a crimper which is a thing that actually puts the bullet part onto the cartridge case. He made all the ammunition; he made a hundred rounds and obviously used some when he was practising. He had to buy the black powder, buy the cases, and the bullet parts. He got some of the stuff from the gunsmith in Ashford where he was a regular customer as he had had a gun licence, which he then lost – but he still bought the ammunition, which was quite interesting.

There were another 16 people on a hit list that he had compiled so I was not alone, but I was the most obvious and easy one. When the list came to light, the police went out and visited everyone on it to see if they were all right. Some people got quite a shock because they had not known that they were on the list. Some had treated his mother in hospital; not all were medical, but most were.

I am one of the few people who had an obituary when I was still alive! Someone rang me up to say, 'Hello Gerry, I hear you are dead.' There had been an article in the Pulse[xxiii] magazine about another guy who was shot two years after me, and they mentioned my name as well 'Dr. Flack, who was shot dead….' I wrote to them to say, 'Well, I am still here.' Consequently, they sent the Cancer Unit at the William Harvey Hospital £250 as compensation for this.

BMA parries violence risk

THE BMA has devised a training package for health service staff on how to deal with violence.

Handling Aggression And Violence In The Health Service is divided into 16 stand-alone units.

The association has developed the package, with Pepar Publications, to combat the growing risk of violence to health service staff.

The BMA highlighted incidents of violence, such as the 1993 shooting of Dr Gerald Flack by the son of a patient who had died.

It estimated that one GP in five GPs was the victim of personal attack that year.

Janet Maguire, BMA indus- ... Thames region, devised the package with Willie More of Pepar.

Ms Maguire said: 'The idea is to allow people to dip into the modules, which are devised to be simple and can be taught in one-hour sessions.'

Health staff could work through only the modules they found most relevant.

The pack, which is aimed at all health service staff, was also aimed at ensuring employers met the requirement under health and safety laws to provide a safe environment.

Ms Maguire explained: 'We realise that this pack cannot stop violent incidents, but it will help provide staff with some techniques to deal with the situation.'

Dr Gerald Flack: Shot dead by the son of a patient who had died

Doctor Magazine 0181 - 652 5738

Above: Newspaper article on my death after the shooting

Right: My response to the article

FURTHER NORTHFIELD
BILTING
ASHFORD
KENT
TN25 4 HD

3 October 1995

The Editor
Doctor Magazine

FAX NO: 0181 652 8701

Dear Sir

The report of my death in your magazine (with colour picture of "reincarnation" with wife) has been somewhat exaggerated. Shot in 1993 - yes, dead - no. Your report has caused my family and colleagues much surprise and amusement. They had supposed that they had seen me enjoying my retirement, in the garden, walking the dogs, tending the sheep and paying the occasional visit to local hostelries, in addition to sitting behind a desk doing the odd locum.

You can imagine the severe distress caused by my premature demise. This must have a valuation in law and I suggest you consult your legal department for an out of court settlement or "non death grant". It could be forwarded to me for a donation to my favourite charity which at the moment is the new cancer day care centre being built at the William Harvey Hospital in Ashford.

Moral - never believe anything you see in print.

With best wishes.

From a very lively (so I am told!)

DR GERALD STAUNTON FLACK

Shot doctor is alive and well

Madam, The report of my death in your newspaper (with colour picture of 'reincarnation' with wife) has been somewhat exaggerated (28 September, page 10).

Shot in 1993 — yes. Dead — no. Your report has caused my family and colleagues much surprise and amusement.

They had supposed they had seen me enjoying my retirement, in the garden, walking the dogs, tending the sheep and paying the occasional visit to local hostelries, in addition to sitting behind a desk doing the odd locum.

You can imagine the severe distress caused by my premature demise. This must have a valuation in law and I suggest you consult your legal department regarding an out-of-court settlement or 'non-death grant'.

It could be forwarded to me for donation to my favourite charity — which at the moment is the cancer day care centre being built at the William Harvey Hospital in Ashford.

Moral — never believe anything you see in print.

With best wishes, from a very lively (so I am told)

Dr Gerald Flack, Ashford, Kent

Editor replies: We are pleased to donate a sum to Dr Flack's favourite charity and apologise for the mistake

Dr Gerald Flack ... report of his death was an error

CHAPTER 20: THE MOVE TO OXENTURN ROAD

It was now time to move on. It had become clear that we had outgrown the original surgery and, despite two expansions, we needed to take the big decision - a move to entirely new premises. And that of course led to all kinds of problems - not least the intricate web of planning and the time it takes.

In 25 years patient number s had increased from 3,000 to 7,000 and the demographics had changed vastly. With transport no longer a problem and patients able to drive to the surgery we were able to expand and increase our facilities. We needed much more space, including much more secretarial space in a big way, as opposed to the one little room in the old surgery. We decided that the thing to do was to go on expanding and to build something rather bigger than we wanted so that we would not have to extend again, as this had been the biggest problem that we had. There were four doctors when we moved to Oxenturn Road and four when I left.

Getting the site for the new surgery was an absolute nightmare. I think that there were seven possible options. We went to the Council and they offered us one site which was next door to the public loos in Churchfield Way. The surgery and loos could go together. That was that with that one, it could have been vandalised. There was another site which earmarked down at the bottom of Churchfield Way but it was in a field there that flooded, so it would have had to have been on stilts. Another one was offered by Mr Sunley up at Withersdane where he was going to develop the field, one of the old hop fields on the way up to Withersdane on the right- hand side. He had hoped to develop it by putting in post graduate houses. Building the surgery there could have supported the consent for development, but this was too far for village patients to walk. There were other smaller sites.

But then, out of the blue, I got rung up by a farmer, Jack Long of Lower Withersdane, and Betty, his wife. Trish used to push prams around with her. They had lived near 'the mayor of Wye', Lordy Holland. They were all part of the Long family. Betty Long rang up to say that they were leaving, to move to Scotland. They had decided that they were selling up their farm here so that they could buy three times as much land in Scotland. So they went up there, and young Long, the son of Jack, was going to farm it with his Dad who had had a minor stroke. As they were going, they said, 'Look, we gather that you are looking for a piece of land for a surgery. Are you interested in this?' I said I was very interested, it sounded ideal. At that time they gave me a price and I said that this sounded more than reasonable. But it got into the hands of an Estate Agent in Ashford who then put a 'realistic' price on it because it was going to be a surgery and doctors could afford it and all that sort of thing, and before we knew it, it went from whatever it was to quite a lot of money. But the site did give us an extra bit of land at the back for expansion, or as a car park, or whatever, so we had more than we needed. So that is how that came about – through Betty Long.

The new surgery at Oxenturn Road under construction

The partners took it in turns at weekends to travel around looking at new surgeries, because suddenly the Government had found new ways of helping practices with the building funding. We did not use the money from the Little Chequers surgery because that was in the name of Ian and myself, and totally separate. We got a loan that was available for general practice surgeries. There was a good repayment on the rent; there were all kinds of repayment schemes available. Funnily enough the place where they starting building the best surgeries was in Norfolk. There were some very smart surgeries, rural ones which were just the design that we wanted; so we did get a lot of ideas by visiting there. We went up to see one that had a very good plan. Oxenturn Road surgery was influenced by it very much and adopted the idea of having brickwork inside rather than plastering. (The surgery has needed hardly any radical maintenance since.) The architect had to insist on building the cement pillars on the outside at the surgery entrance, which I was dead against, because if he had put these up as brick it would have been plagiarism of the surgery in Norfolk. It was close to it. (That was the one thing that I have got against that surgery building, the cement pillars outside.) It will go on for years because there is an enormous amount of space upstairs. The top floor was converted into a one-bedroomed flat and next to it a large conference room. Then there is the roof space, which is also enormous, which we had boarded etc. and has now has been extended into offices.

The move to Oxenturn Road happened at a time when we had another Doctor and Roz Waller was, about that time, made, an 'assistant with a view'. The whole system of taking on partners changed enormously during the years. Doctors used to start most commonly as 'assistant without a view'. Later the offer was for partnership in six years, and by the end it had reduced to six months.

Top left: The new Surgery with field behind

Above: The new Surgery from the front

Left: The new Surgery Practice Manager, Ann Seniot and Dispenser, Hazel Harris with Lincoln long-wools

Equality came very quickly. It became very hard to get a partner, whereas before it was not. If you read the book 'General Practice Under the National Health Service 1948 –1997[xxiv] it gives the exact timing and the attitude of both the consultants to the GPs, and GPs to the consultants, and all the changes that occurred over a period of 50 years. For the actual change, we had incentives for building new surgeries with regard to interest-free loans and so on, and, as we said, we went around investigating the other surgeries that had been built in Norfolk and Suffolk.

The new surgery had better facilities for a secretarial working area behind the reception and a proper pharmacy and treatment room. There was a Health Visitor's room and a Nurse's room. There was a small room for Minor Surgery that was attached to the nurses' treatment room. There was also a field behind the surgery on which we put sheep. We thought that this was the way that general practice was going. The surgery was built before Practice Managers were introduced, though this happened before I left. Originally it was Ann Senior, who had been with us for years as a secretary. I am pretty sure that a surgeon still came out from Canterbury at the start.

When I took the practice over in 1964 I did not like the idea of prescribing and having our own pharmacy. There was a chemist in the village, the Co-op Chemist, Mr Skinner, a super chap and a really good fellow. He had an assistant a very nice Scots lady, Mrs Foster, who was the wife of the Clerk of Works to the College. The pharmacy was opposite the College; it later became Geerings and then a bookshop. (Mr Skinner was an authority on orchids. That was his hobby and he took me out to see orchids on my half days occasionally. We once went over to Fred Richardson and his sister Ruth's home in Hassell Street and they took us to see lady orchids, butterfly orchids and wintergreen – very appropriate.)

Anyway, it seemed wrong to me that there should be a village pharmacist and us. Rural practices were allowed to carry on prescribing under the national health scheme, so we could prescribe and get paid for it. This would cut out his living and also I found this a bind, to be quite honest. Not only did we have to make up the medicines and get all the stuff in and so on, but there were certain things that he stocked and we did not, so it was all very confusing. So I applied to give up prescribing, which we did. So Mr Skinner then did all the prescribing and the Co-op Chemist thrived.

But then later on when the practice was growing and growing, the policy changed and we thought we had better prescribe because we could not pay for ourselves. So we re-applied and there were a lot of objections from the Co-op obviously, but we started prescribing again. That was when the new Oxenturn Surgery was built. I was not prescribing in the Little Chequers Surgery because there was not really room. We could do weekend prescribing and emergency prescribing and had enough stocks for this, but the new surgery gave us the facility to prescribe and that is when we started again. That was when the proper pharmacy was built and it had to be secure and meet other regulations.

Interestingly enough, at the very beginning, we thought about applying to be fund-holders, but our practice was too small. You had to have 9,000 or 10,000 plus patients. We only had 7,500 or 8,000 patients, so we would have been turned down. The next thing they were suddenly saying was that they were looking for small surgeries to fund-hold, and so we applied again, and we were told this time that we were too big! Eventually, it was open to everybody, so we applied and got the fund-holding. That was classic.

When we were fundholding, (rather like the wheel has been invented again), I think that we continued to call the hospital consultants out to the surgery. The surgery was also used for sessional counsellors, hearing tests, eye tests and other things as well. There was enough room for all of this and still is. The surgeons and sessional staff were paid by us as becoming fund-holders enabled this.

The income of the practice was based on a per capita payment and could be augmented by extra money. For example, Ian Nash did one day a week at the Batchelors factory, which all were benefiting from. If any work was done in 'ordinary time', it went into the kitty and 'ordinary time' was when you were on call. We did charge some Police work though, allowing each of us to keep the payment when we were called out, but obviously we also got a retainer, a lump sum, for the police work, and that went into the practice, as did my seniority payment (maybe £5,000 a year) which I waived and it went back into the kitty.

When we had been on holiday to Canada in the 1970's, the doctors' talk was always about finance and how to make more money through property or how they were working and this was their big thing. That convinced us that we had done the right thing in staying here because we were practising medicine - family medicine - and our pals over in Canada changed. They would never go out of their way. Over there in Canada medicine has changed to finance-led interventions and they also had no relationships other than with their medical colleagues. I found that, provided one worked and enjoyed the job and so on, eventually along the line the money followed afterwards. We started off absolutely screwed but then, as time went on, financially we did improve. Not to any fantastic extent, but here we are. We have been very fortunate. The government changes in GP payment policies are purely political. They were negotiated for us and one wonders about the negotiators because they probably opted out of pure medicine with patients quite early on in their careers.

In 1989, I celebrated my 60th birthday. I could have lived without a change because I felt that I was on to a good thing with the partners because there were four of us who shared the work so we only had one weekend on in four – it was luxury really from what I was used to. It was not a problem for the practice to be covering 365 days, but I knew that as soon as we gave it up, GPs would really walk over the Labour Government. Eventually they got absolutely everything they wanted in their 2004 revised GP contracts . But what they also got was a massive bureaucracy on top of them, watching every move – which they brought on themselves really. They no longer look after themselves. In my time, I was an independent contractor, but I am not sure that they are now. We were self employed, but it is all very different now. We were only accountable to ourselves and to our patients. We had a contract with the patient.

My 60th Birthday

Ian Nash was very good at managing. Then there was a junior practice manager who came in. She had gone through a course on 'how to be a practice manager' through a university somewhere. I think that that side of the practice was very well run and it provided a system that would be ongoing. Ian felt that he should have protected time to be responsible for the management side of things at least once a week and, in fact, that was one of the resentments. I thought that this was very fair as it was important to know where the organisation was, and we needed to see that the practice was going in the right direction, not only practically, but also financially; but this was one of the problems.

Another of the problems was outside practice activities. For example, the Police Surgeon work was primarily a nocturnal activity. The Police just called us out, often at night. If you did get to attend during the day you could be out for a long time and others had to cover for you. I think one had accepted that this was part of working life, but it was not accepted so easily by somebody new coming in who had not been brought up with it.

The same with the K.A.R.E.S scheme. There was unhappiness with it. I think that a lot of the trainee doctors had not had to do a casualty department slot. They had done surgery and they had done medicine, and probably something like a paediatrics slot, but avoided casualty or emergency medicine which really was the thing that we were involved in by going out to the roadside. (I gave a talk to 15 or 20 trainees in Canterbury and only one had done any casualty work and he was also the only one to have done a First Aid course!) Having said that, the scheme was not just dealing with the roadside emergencies, it was the same equipment that you needed for emergencies in the home or in the garden or for anything else. So the attitude was that it was for outside work, road accidents etc., but it was not just that, emergency medicine was needed 'homeside' as well as 'roadside'. We ran both K.A.R.E.S. and were police surgeons with just four GPs. All did equal nights on and off.

At that time in the Practice it sometimes felt as if we had become two groups, the 'oldies' and the 'young'. The 'oldies' wanted to keep everything going. To be fair, I think what happened was that when I was there, there were two young and two old – this happens in any business. It kept a balance then - we were chivvied below and they were sat on from above, so that worked, funnily enough; but because we 'oldies' were more experienced, we obviously held the sway. You get change but it is slow, it is not a revolution, it is an evolution.

Later, when I left, it seemed to me, that the then three young partners made life difficult for Ian and Ian's right hand person who was the Practice Manager. As Ian said, 'no one would work as Gerry and I worked and the whole of that has ramifications on the rest of it'. So it was three against two. That is as one saw it from the outside. Ann Senior departed when GP fund-holding ended. She had been the fund-holding manager. Ian also decided to leave, and took over the police work afterwards. It was very hard and I found it very difficult because not only was Ian a long- term partner of mine but he was also a good friend and has always been 'Ian'. We had not needed to discuss things, we knew exactly what each other would have wanted to do. He does not change. We found that tough. This was the way it happened. It was not just at Wye, it was everywhere.

Trish got fed up with me because when we were driving around past a house I would say who was in it and what had happened. I have memories just like that, it is funny, I am pretty useless at remembering people's names, but places and incidents are as clear as clear. I went somewhere on Saturday and a lady came up to me and said 'you do not remember me, but...' and I said 'no I do not, but...' and then I said, 'I do remember you. You lived along the road in a bungalow. Are you still living there?' and I remembered absolutely in detail the incident which was about 30 years ago. And she said 'you told me that if ever I fly I had always to put on very tight socks because I might get deep vein thrombosis. I have been to America and I did what you said'.

I was looking at the well-known individuals I had met over the years. Did I mention Lord Hailsham?[xxvi] He was down for the shooting at the Loudon's at Olantigh and they had a tractor and trailer pulling people around from one stand to another. He was on a straw bale at the back of the trailer and fell off and landed on his backside and bruised himself. They thought that he had broken his back, so I was called to see him. His son, Douglas Hogg, also a politician, was hopping around in a right state saying he ought to go to hospital before I had even seen him. I examined Lord Hailsham, who was charming, and we discussed it. He was obviously bruised and had damaged his coccyx. He was very straightforward and he said, "Well, I have got to attend parliament tomorrow," and we discussed that it would not be comfortable sitting on his Wool ack! Actually, the traditional treatment was a rubber ring!

The big thing was that he was not a patient of mine, and as such he had to become a temporary resident and needed to sign a form. Of course, he had no idea what a temporary resident was or about the forms because they normally went to Harley Street or somewhere or people came to see them and sent the bill in at the end of the month. So he was educated about the Health Scheme at the same time. The same happened once when I got called to Eastwell Manor with one of the Sainsburys who was in Government in some role and they had no idea about the health scheme at all.

I looked after a family called Broderick in Eastwell Manor before it was bought by developers and turned into an hotel. When I visited them, Captain Broderick took me to see Mrs Broderick who was in bed. In those days beds always had an eiderdown on the top. In my bedside manner, I sat on the eiderdown and underneath there was a great squirm and a dachshund emerged. So that put me off my stroke a bit. After that, whenever I did home visits I used to pat the eiderdown and some people said 'what are you doing' and I had to explain why

Eastwell Manor

I did it and, of course, it was a good way of breaking the ice with a sick patient because they thought it was hilarious. The trouble was, as time went on, there were very few beds that you could sit on as they became divan beds and so much lower, so then you had to get down on your knees to patients. I also had a cartilage that used to trouble me, and I could not get up sometimes. I had to kick my leg to try to straighten myself out. There was also a problem for home deliveries with divan beds, we had to put blocks under the legs to get them to a reasonable height. The midwives used to take blocks around with them.

My dear old Marianne was about seven, and birthday parties were in and all the kids would have them. There was a party at The Saracen's Head Hotel in Ashford. It no longer exists, it was where Boots is now on the corner. I was on call, and on the Saturday afternoon there was this party. I drove Marianne there and took her in. I knew that I still had some more visits to do on my way back to Wye when I got stopped in Kennington – I was doing over 30 mph. I was represented at court by the AA and got fined. A while after this, I went to see Mrs Broderick and the gallant Captain, who was also a JP. He took me down for a glass of sherry or something. He stood with his back to the fire and said, 'oh you must be more careful driving, Flack'. (I was called Flack, that was how it was, I was addressed as 'Flack'.) 'You really must be more careful, Flack'. That I kept in my mind. Eventually, after some years, on a particular occasion in the thick, heavy snow, his wife was taken quite ill and was having to be transferred up to London by ambulance. The ambulance could not get to Eastwell's front door, so was down at the gate. I had a little Ford Anglia. I think that I had some snow tyres on it and managed to drive carefully and cautiously right the way round to the front door and to dear, old Broderick, who was not a very fit man. Mrs Broderick was upstairs and not at all well, there was nobody else in the place; it was an enormous place with only the two of them in it with a couple of Portuguese helps, that was all – it was sad when you think about it. So I carried Mrs. Broderick down the stairs because her husband was in such a state and put her in my car. He got in the back and we drove round to the ambulance and they put her in the ambulance and off she went. After that, he thought about it, and said, 'I have known you long enough now, Flack, my name is George' and I said, 'Well, mine's Gerald'.

But there was a sequel to all of this, a worse one actually. His son Julian was at school in Dorset. Broderick went down to collect him for half term and on the way back, poor old Julian, who was in the back of the car, was terribly sick all over a cushion. So George pulled up in some village and got this cushion, which was covered in vomit, tossed it nonchalantly over a hedge. Behind the hedge was a bloke who was mowing his grass and he shouted 'here' rushed out and saw this Rolls Royce driving off, and reported it. When I next visited Eastwell, George was apoplectic because he had been fined. So I said 'Well George, you have been in trouble lately, I see. You must be more careful!' He had to give up being a JP.

Another person who came our way was a chap called Nicholas Tolstoy who was a student at the time. A family called Wicksted who lived in Bridge Street, Wye, looked after him. They lived next to Maxted's the butchers, and then they moved to Kennington. They were in *loco parentis* to the two Tolstoys, Nicholas and his sister, Natasha. Nicholas was under my care for a while with a severe bad back. He had a rare condition, but got on successfully in life. He later did a degree in Dublin and became a successful author and an historian. He then fell foul of Lord Aldington because he accused him of war atrocities through being complicit in the white Cossacks being sent back to Russia. They were all shot when they got back – it upset me terribly. It was a big legal case and Tolstoy lost it. I am a bit cynical about this because I think that the establishment was against him.

There was a Miss Weigall who lived in Scotton Street. Her father was an artist and sculptor and had painted and sculpted Wellington – one of his portraits is in the National Portrait Gallery. This fine old lady, Miss Weigall, who must have been in her late 80s, had lived in Walmer-cum-Deal. She told me how when she was four or five she had been for lunch one day with a chap called Sebag Montefiore, a well-known name; I believe theirs was the first Jewish family to get a commission in the British army. A whole lot of kids were invited as it was his 90th birthday. She told me 'yes, and we were all given a medal to celebrate it. What he told us was that, when he was a young man, he had had lunch on the Victory with Lord Nelson when he was at Chatham in the Dockyard in 1802'. There was I sitting there beside her when she was in bed and she said, 'that is the medal there on the wall, doctor'. So I was sitting there with a direct contact with Nelson. When she died, she left me a parian bust of Wellington. It is in the dining room. In fact, one day I went to the National Portrait Gallery, and sure enough there is a portrait of Wellington by Weigall in the gallery.

Funnily enough, by sheer chance, when I was soldiering at Mons Barracks, I was queuing up to report and it was, 'next, next' , and 'name': '2055606, Flack,

Sir', to the sergeant and the next one was Sebag Montefiore, and the sergeant who was letting us all in said, 'ahh, Sebag Montefiore, we have been waiting for you'. The poor chap was picked out because he was short. He was a lovely fellow. I think that either he is the writer or his son is the writer. They are quite a family of writers. Somebody is always picked out in the army to be in the middle of the front rank as a point of reference. So when we were all in a row it was always, 'three men to the right of Montefiore' – he was the reference point for everything.

Visit by the Queen Mother meeting the community outside Wye Church

In about 1984, when the Queen Mother visited Wye College at Withersdane, I was the official doctor and was introduced to her. There is a photo of all my family there at the time. When she came out of the Church there was a row of elderly ladies sitting outside on chairs. The Queen Mother talked to them and shook hands with them. One said afterwards that she was never going to wash her hands again. One of the ladies had told the Queen Mother that Boughton Aluph had the second longest living residents in the country. She said back, 'actually they live a long time where I come from'. Another time I had to go to the Sports Ground to await the arrival of a helicopter, but the only one who landed was the Lord Lieutenant, so I hid under a tree with my black bag.

MP Keith Speed was at school with me. He left school aged 15 and went to Dartmouth to train as a naval officer. When he became MP for Ashford under the Thatcher government he was put in charge of the navy. His claim to fame was that he was sacked from his post for arguing against reducing the navy. I remember a speech he made in Tenterden – he particularly objected to removing the patrol boat around the Falklands. He lived in Wye and I got to know him then. His wife said that when she went back with him to Admiralty House to clear his office – it was at the top of a spiral staircase – he was clapped all the way down again.

Joanna Lumley was a patient for a while when she was living with the Armitage family in Eggarton Lane. She met her husband through the family. She remained friendly with the Armitages and the Wards in particular, and has continued to be very supportive of local events.

Sir Edward Hardy, ex-Governor of Wye College, lived in Chilham Castle. He was a real gentleman and was very good to his farm workers. He and Reg Older were partners in Penstock Farms. He later lived at Boughton Court. Another chap was Viscount Massereene and Ferrard who lived at Chilham Castle. He had two daughters. One of them, Sheila, married an Irishman and the other, Oriel, later worked at Eastwell Manor as organiser.

Stanley Christopherson lived at Spring Grove, Wye (before it became a school). He was a hero of the Second World War whose 'Wartime Diaries' are often quoted. He had decided to cultivate 'rare breed ducks'. Unfortunately he didn't reckon with the local mallards destroying his bloodstock. His wife, Cynthia, asked me what they could do about it and I recommended Fred Catt to sort them out as he was the best poacher around. One day he was asked to deal with two drakes causing havoc in their pond. So, as I heard later, Fred, having been called out, disappears into the reeds, and he is gone for a very long time. 'He was there so long, I didn't know what was going on,' said Cynthia. Eventually there was one shot and out comes Freddy with the two birds. 'Why did it take you so long?' asked Cynthia. 'I had to wait a long time to get them both in the same shot,' said Fred. As a poacher, he could only manage a single shot before attracting attention.

CHAPTER 22: THE DECISION TO RETIRE 1994

My retirement was just because of my age, 65. I had done 40 years. Actually, I had not, I had done 39 years, but I discovered a clause that my national service as a registered medical student, counted. When I went into the army, I filled in as occupation, 'medical student' and so my student time had been interfered with and this counted as half-time for the health service and it added up, so I was able to have the full pension.

I did not retire because I was shot which is what people said, but it was about a year after that I think. I retired because I was 65 but I must say that I think that I was finding it a little difficult – the computer scene was not my thing somehow. To be honest I am not good at paperwork and am more or less computer illiterate. I could get the name up, and basic things, but not a lot more and I was not happy. It seemed to me that the whole system was coming between me and communication and I found this not easy. To be honest, I am used to looking a patient in the eye when they are talking to me, to see if they are pulling the wool over my eyes or whether they are covering something up. To me, this was an important part of the consultation, the diagnosis, and the choice of treatment. The coming of computers meant that I could not look them in the eye as I had to be looking at the wretched screen on my desk. I had thought of retiring at 60, but decided to stay on for the stability of the practice. This was, in principle true, actually, especially when somebody like David Marriott told Trish that he went to see a nameless doctor, and they said what is the trouble, and he said something like, 'the pills you gave me last time are not suiting me'. The doctor got out his pharmacy guide and looked through it and typed something out on the computer and then he turned round to the 'patient' and said 'oh, it is you Canon Marriott, I did not realise'.

It was time to retire, there were too many changes taking place, dividing the practice into two, with pressure from the young – 'Vocation with strings attached'. The desire to opt out of the 365 days/year responsibility was growing. GP contracts were changing. During my last year, a letter came from CEDoc and that gave the practice the opportunity to opt out of 24/7 care. Over my dead body. Retirement was therefore a natural consequence. It was the right time. Ian Nash carried on after me at the practice. Ian was the boss of the practice after I left and then it was Roz Waller.

Trish was still working. She worked nights and made her pension up. It is very interesting because although I retired from Wye, I still did locums for another five or six years. I said when I retired, 'Look, I am not going to work here and I am not going to do any work at all for six months.' I did do one locum in Wye because they all had to go to a special meeting or something and had a day out. I went in and said, 'You are not to say that I am doing a locum.' I was just hidden and did one day's surgery. It was extraordinary because I did a visit on that day to a farmer whose wife was suddenly taken acutely ill. I went out to see them in the morning. I knew how ill she was and said to the farmer that I would pop back. I did the surgery in the afternoon and then went back again afterwards and she died whilst I was there. I had known them all the time that I had been at Wye surgery and the wife frequently had to go to St Augustine's. He was the carer, a wonderful man. I thought, 'how the heck am I going to say this' and he said to me 'I know what you are going to say, doctor, I am glad that she went first'. That was exactly what I was going to say to him, but not in those basic words. If he had gone first it would have been a disaster. I had saved his life several years previously when he was stung by bees.

Another beekeeper had been Professor Schwabe in Bilting, who persisted in keeping bees despite having severe allergic reaction to the stings. After two emergencies, I supplied him with a syringe and drugs to do it himself.

Doing locums rejuvenated me. I did them at Chilham, Ham Street, and other rural practices. One in Folkestone, though, I did not repeat. Appointments there were restricted to five minutes only and I found it impossible to do a good job when faced by an old couple with multiple problems. Generally I was fortunate in that every practice had a different computer system and so, at the end of the day I would borrow a secretary for half an hour and would dictate the notes. I did Monday evenings at Chilham surgery for about five years after I retired.

Below left: Trish and I on my retirement

Below: Our Golden Wedding

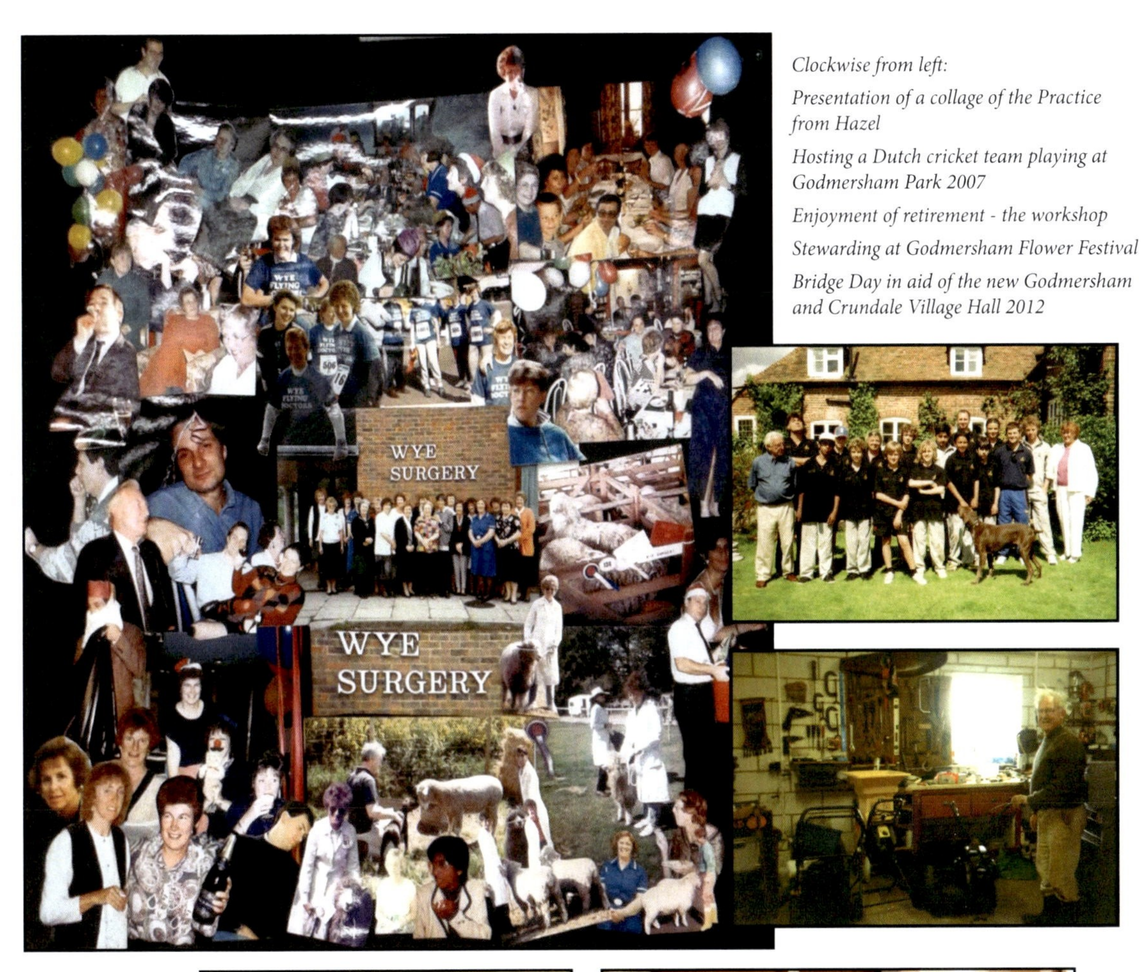

Clockwise from left:

Presentation of a collage of the Practice from Hazel

Hosting a Dutch cricket team playing at Godmersham Park 2007

Enjoyment of retirement - the workshop

Stewarding at Godmersham Flower Festival

Bridge Day in aid of the new Godmersham and Crundale Village Hall 2012

CHAPTER 23: RETROSPECTIVE AND REFLECTIONS

People who have influenced me before I started medicine were Dr Hughes, whom I have mentioned, and a school master, Billy Belcher who had been my house master and acted more or less in loco parentis for my father when I was there. After all, I spent more time at school than the holidays, if you think about it. My 'guardians' who brought me up probably influenced me more than anybody. In medicine I was influenced by the Balfours from whom I learned to give time to patients. They had an attitude that was worth following. There were a hell of a lot of patients who also impressed me – usually at the end of their days which was always terribly sad. You get to know them extraordinarily well, particularly when making them the last visits of the day on the way home; one got to know people very well then and they were prepared to talk.

One of these was Dr. Francis Richards FRS[xxvii] who had been Director of the Agricultural Research Council (ARC) Morphogenesis and Nutrition Unit at Rothamstead. He moved to Wye when the unit, which was dependent on his research leadership, was transferred to the College. He had hardly arrived at Wye before he got cancer. I looked after him throughout his illness. The only thing that was in his mind was to find all the staff who were affected, new jobs. He lived in Oxenturn Road on the left hand side. He managed to find them all places in England and then he died. He was an agnostic or whatever but he had it all totally sussed out – if one could die like that, one could die happy. He was a great influence on me.

I do not think that I ever really thought about being a GP in terms of my philosophy. It was a vocation. The vocations were the Church, teaching, medicine, and lawyers might claim it. But we have all now given it up as a vocation, it is just a job now. That is the change that I see. I had not expected it to be anything but a vocation when I went in for it. It was a family concern and we just accepted it. Patients came first and family came second. This has been one of the things learned later on from the children, 'every time we were about to go out, Dad, something happened, again and again'. School events I did not get to. I used to do the obstetrics in the practice when we first came because of a slight difference of opinion with Dr Balfour on the use of chloroform, so it meant that if anybody went into labour, I had to be around. We were going to go to Heathrow to see the aeroplanes to give the kids a day out. You can guess, somebody went into labour at Spring Grove farm in Harville Road, Amos's farm. One of the farm worker's wives started to have her baby. I said to the family 'sorry, but I have to go to deal with this'. This was at 8 am in the morning and by 10 am she was delivered and well again. So our trip was delayed and by the time that we got there, half the day was missed. I have not forgotten it – nor have the family.

"Patients first" was the philosophy of some of my contemporaries, but the difference was reinforced when a lot of them went to Canada in the early 1960s. There was a tremendous emigration of doctors, GPs in particular, because of the difficulties of getting into practices at all. We did not go, but as when we went over to Canada eventually in 1973 for a holiday, it was quite obvious that their attitude was not a vocation at all, it was as things are now, it was the 'bucks'. It was a private system, and 'real estate' was the thing.

I was also slightly influenced, by the army. When you are in the army, the first thing you do is to look after your troops, see that they are watered and fed and then you can sit down. Troops first, yourself second, and then it is you who won't get shot in the back! It was the tradition of the First World War. I think that was the attitude. I felt the same really, patients first, staff second ourselves third. I do not mean the family because that was up to me, but it affected the family. Perhaps that is being big headed? Trish remembered that planned weekends away sometimes had to be cancelled. If you had been invited for a weekend with friends and you could not go because I was on duty. That was hard. People who were not in medicine found it difficult to understand. They did not understand when they came to stay with us that I was on call. Trish's father was the worst. 'Why can't they b. well wait?' I remember one Christmas, with a chap over at Yockletts. He had a heart attack. I was called out in the middle of Christmas dinner and did not come back until 4 pm. People could not understand that patients went ill anytime, not just according to working hours. Other people do have rather set hours.

In the earlier days, because our facilities and treatments were so sparse, one tended to visit much more frequently and the follow-ups were very important in order to see if somebody was getting better after what you had done, or not, because there were no guarantees. People stayed at home when they had their heart attacks and they were six weeks in bed. That was traditional and totally wrong until somebody recognised that people who got up and wandered around lived longer. Then the whole thing changed and then you were in trouble because people would say 'when my Dad had a heart attack, he was in bed for six weeks' – meaning you are taking me out of my bed doctor.

Finally, vicars and I often visited the same people. After I had retired, I met the Reverend Finch, vicar of Hastingleigh and Elmstead. He said, 'I have been looking forward to meeting you'. We were visiting the same person, an old woodsman in Crundale. He had been told to stay in bed and it was hard to keep him there. When the vicar had arrived at the house, his dog had barked loudly and he heard a voice shouting down 'Stop that noise you f-ing dog'. When Rev. Finch went upstairs he said to him, 'Oh, I'm sorry vicar, I thought it was the doctor'.

SOME TRIBUTES ON RETIREMENT OF DR. GERRY FLACK 1994

L.P. - Chilham
Many thanks for the care and attention you have given M and myself. I remember especially your kindness in coming to see me within hours of M's dying.

R.M. - Wye
The skill, kindness and friendship which you have given us have been a vital support in the difficult times and have at all times enhanced the pleasure of living in Wye.

J. family - Naccolt
Just a letter to say how much the P. and family appreciate your service to us in the pass not only as a Dr but as a great friend.

P.L. - Wye
The loss of you and David Marriott will be deeply felt. Wye will not be the same without you both to help us in our needs.

R. - Wye
I must confess that latterly I always gave H. a list of the specific things he had to report to you on his health as he so enjoyed gossiping with you that he used to come back, having failed completely to ask you what he had come for!

V.W. - Crundale
I shall miss coming to the surgery full of aches and pains and going out feeling fine (until the next time).

B.S. - Wye
You always had time to listen.

K.B. - Brook
I often think how good you were when you used to come. And also for letting Jill come to look at my ear last year. And ring J.P. every evening to see how she is as I think she will miss you Gerry.

W.H. - Kennington
Very many thanks for your kindness in so many past years.
PS Please let me know when you are ready for your lawn grass seed.

E.W. - Kennington
We shall miss the advice you give, which we know is borne of years of experience, and the homely way it was imparted.

G.C. - Bilting
We specially appreciate the time taken to explain the treatment where possible.

P. - Wye
I'm enclosing a small contribution to your retirement gift. We were asked to write GSF on the envelope and I spent one walk with the dog letting my mind range over possible interpretations of these initials – from the prosaic Gerry's Support Fund, Superannuation . . . The down-to-earth socks, sweaters, septic-tank, snooker table . . . The more adventurous (equipment for) sailing, ski-jumping, sky-diving . . . The exotic – funds for a safari, statue, stock-breeding, sauna, swimming-pool . . . to the desperate Gerry's SOS Fund! . . . When I got home normal rationality returned and I saw from the phone book that your full initials are GSF.

R. - Boughton Lees
You became friend, counsellor, doctor, so many different things to your wide family. Also to say thank you to your family who have had to share you over the years.

J.R. - Challock
Thank you firstly for putting up with all my aches and pains over the years. Your care to patients is phenomenal, especially the time you came out to me at 2.00 a.m. in the morning. You sat and held my hand and reassured me that I wasn't having a heart attack, just a panic attack. You are a sweet man and I will miss you.

J.W. - Kennington
Thank you Gerry and you Trish. We feel privileged to have known, and, at times, needed you as our Doctor over the years. On our first day back after seven years living away, you passed us in your car and we asked 'would you please take us back on your books'. 'I'd be offended if you went elsewhere' came the reply.

R.C. - Hastingleigh
I remember when I had found father lying on the floor, possibly having a heart attack. You came in minutes and unblocked his throat and suddenly he was up and very much alive. You gave your precious time and your life to the care of your patients.

J.D.
You have the wonderful ability of giving the impression that you are not in a hurry and have all the time to listen to your patient's woes.

J.W. - Bilting
..You drove J's car home and locked it up when he had to go to hospital from the surgery. You called to see my Mum one evening at 9.30 pm and sat with her, so we could have something to eat. You gave up lunchtime to come and just be with J's mum.

R.W.
You came one afternoon and stitched up C's injured hand amidst the debris of Sunday lunch. Then there was M. and the noisy removal of her rear stitches. P's appendectomy, K's tonsillectomy, the mysterious illness which proved to be german measles, and gentle support at the end for G. There is much more to thank you for.

H. - Boughton Aluph
Understanding, an extra so appreciated is how we remember Dr Flack. A young, inexperienced mother needed reassurance and problem was put into context. Birth of a son – how did so many squash into the small bedroom – and the dog too?

L. - Bodsham
Life is never going to be the same again. For 34 years it has been a pleasure to feel poorly, even to the point of breaking ones leg.

L.B. - Wye
K... views with paranoid suspicion dentists and surgeons. When he was told he needed to part with his gall bladder, it was to you that he automatically turned and will always be grateful for the time you spent with him explaining the pros and cons of the operation. Gerry, you have opened your door countless times and saved and improved the quality of thousands of lives. Thank you for everything.

FINALLY

At a talk given by Gerry in February 2016 for the Wye Arts Association, at which over 200 people came, this recollection from a patient was included in his introduction by John Rogers:

'When I was newly arrived in the village, I asked my neighbour who the local doctor was'. She said 'the doctor here is Dr. Gerry Flack. Pointing her finger upwards, she continued; 'Up there is God. Just below him, is Gerry Flack'.

Selected by Transcribers

Left: Bilting Palntation with Trish, and Gita and Fleurie our German Shorthaired Pointers.

Above: Why my family called me 'Silverback'.

Below: Flack extended family celebration around 1999.

Above: My family on my 70th birthday.

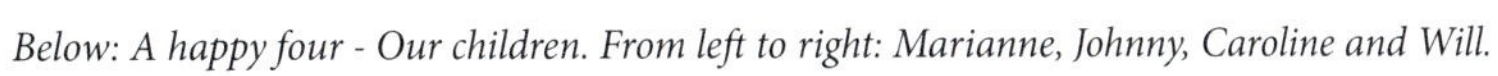

Below: A happy four - Our children. From left to right: Marianne, Johnny, Caroline and Will.

NOTES

[i] 'When I Grow Too Old to Dream' 1934. Composer: Sigmund Romburg. Lyrics: Oscar Hammerstein II. (p.5)

[ii] Sir Thomas Holmes Sellors Surgeon. (p.9)

[iii] (Questions in Parliament: Hansard HC Deb 21 September 1948 vol 456 cc47-50W) (p.10)

[iv] Alan Francis Brooke, 1st Viscount Alanbrooke of Brookeborough, (born July 23, 1883—died June 17, 1963. British field marshal and chief of the Imperial General Staff during World War II. (p.13)

[v] Lady Prudence Loudon late of Olantigh Towers, Wye.) (p.14)

[vi] 'Home, Home on the Range' Lyricist Dr. Brewster M. Higley of Kansas in a poem entitled 'My Western Home' 1872. After 1871,the music was added by Daniel E. Kelley (1843–1905). (p.15)

[vii] Dame Cicely Mary Saunders OM DBE FRCS FRCP FRCN (22 June 1918 – 14 July 2005). Founder of the first modern hospice St. Christoher's in 1967. (p.16)

[viii] L'Arche is an International Federation dedicated to the creation and growth of homes, programs, and support networks with people who have intellectual disabilities.(p.16)

[ix] Group Captain Geoffrey Leonard Cheshire, Baron Cheshire VC, OM, DSO & Two Bars, DFC (7 September 1917 – 31 July 1992). He founded a hospice that grew into the charity Leonard Cheshire Disability (p.16)

[x] Michael O'Donnell (born 20 October 1928). Is a British physician, journalist, author, and broadcaster. He became a full-time writer after working for 12 years as a doctor. On BBC Radio Four he chaired 'My Word' (p.19)

[xi] President Craveiro Lopes of Portugal (12 April 1894 – 2 September 1964) politician and military man. He was the 12th President of the Portuguese Republic between 1951 and 1958.(p.20)

[xii] West Kent Hospital Maidstone closed in 1982 when new Maidstone Hospital was opened (p.22)

[xiii] All Saints Hospital Chatham was formerly Medway Union Workhouse.It was, until 1999, the main maternity and geriatric hospital for the Medway Towns. It was closed in 2001.(p.23)

[xiv] Lloyd George Scheme: Introduced by Liberal Chancellor of the Exchequer, David Lloyd George (1908–1915), within the 1911 National Insurance Act, providing British workers with insurance against illness and unemployment for small compulsory weekly contribution. (p.34)

[xv] William Henry Beveridge, 1st Baron Beveridge KCB (5 March 1879 – 16 March 1963). British economist, noted progressive, and social reformer. Best known for his 1942 Beveridge Report which was the basis for the welfare state put in place by the Labour government elected in 1945. (p.34)

[xvi] Aneurin Bevan (15 November 1897 – 6 July 1960), often known as Nye Bevan, was a Welsh Labour Party politician who was the post-war Minister for Health 1945-51 under the Atlee Government (p.34)

[xvii] Wye College 1894 – 2009. Started as South Eastern Agricultural College 1884. Became School of Agriculture of the federal London University 1898. 1902 granted degree awarding powers. Merged with Imperial College 2000. Closed by Imperial College 2009 (p.51)

[xviii] John Stanton Ward CBE (10 October 1917 - 13 June 2007) was an English portrait artist, landscape painter and illustrator. His subjects included British royalty and celebrities (p.52).

[xix] 'Leaves from Our Tuscan Kitchen', or How to Cook Vegetables (Cookery Library): Janet Ross, Michael Waterfield. Published by Penguin Books Ltd 01/11/1990 (p.61)

[xx] In 1965 GPs demanded a new contract and threatened mass resignation from the NHS. One of their complaints was that there was no provision for improvement of practices. The main problem, however, was in comparison to the pay and status of hospital consultants (p.66)

[xxi] The new payment system, known as the Red Book, allowed doctors to claim back from the NHS 70% of staff costs and 100% of the cost of their premises. Maternity Services and contraception were optional services which attracted additional payments. GPs were allowed to practise privately although few did. (p.66)

[xxii] Rev Dr. Stanley Graham Brade-Birks D.Sc. 1887 – 1992. Canon and Scientist. Dr Brade-Birks took up a lectureship at the South Eastern Agricultural College, Wye, Kent, in 1919. In 1930, he was installed as Vicar Godmersham Parish and later as Rector of Crundale. In 1924. he was awarded as D. Sc. of the University of London for his work on the economic status of Myriapoda.

[xxiii] Pulse is a monthly news magazine and website on British primary care, distributed free to GPs in the UK since 1960. Its stories are regularly picked up by national and regional newspapers.

[xxiv] National Health Service 1948-1997 (1998). Loudon, I. Jorder, J. and Webster, C. Clarendon Press, Oxford (p.112).

[xxvi] Quintin Hogg, Lord Hailsham (1907-2001), was a Conservative frontbencher and Cabinet Minister for more than 30 years, a semi-permanent fixture of the political scene who contrived, nonetheless, never to pass unnoticed.

[xxvii] Dr. Francis John Richards FRS (1st October 1901 – 2 January 1964). Research Institute of Plant Physiology Imperial College (1926-58) Director of new Agricultural Research Unit of Plant Morphogenesis and Nutrition at Rothamsted, which later moved to Wye. Elected a member of the Royal Society in 1954.

ACKNOWLEDGEMENTS

I owe the existence of this book to the persistence of my wife Trish, who was keen for me to make a record of my life. She passed on her strong wish to Sally Leaver, who oversaw the recordings and presented Trish with a first draft of the transcript just days before she died. It was her promise to Trish that impelled Sally to "carry on nagging", alongside the quiet persuasion of Roz Field, until the job was done.

Thanks go to my four children and the extended family for their support and encouragement and to my wonderful patients and colleagues, without whom this would be a very slim volume.

My thanks to Ian Benson, Roz Field and, particularly, to Sally Leaver, for many hours of recording, transcribing, checking and supporting research. Also to Andy Day at Mickle Creative.

Others who have helped include:

Additional contributions:

Marion Balfour
Dorothy Coulter
Dr Ian Nash
Gladys Smith

Comprehension edit:

Pam Rogers

Photographs:

Maureen De Saxe - Wye Historical Society
Ian Cooling
Dorothy Coulter
Alan Paterson
Anne Sutherland

Publishers:

Mickle Print (Canterbury) Ltd